I0605938

FASTER THAN A JET, BIGGER THAN A WHALE

HELVETIQ publishing has been supported by the Swiss Federal Office of Culture with a structural grant for the years 2021–2025.

This book has been translated thanks to a contribution awarded by the Italian Ministry of Foreign Affairs and International Cooperation.

Faster than a Jet, Bigger than a Whale
An Illustrated Guide to Measuring Our World

Originally published as:
Le Misure del Mondo
Natura, animali, uomini e costruzioni a confronto

www.giunti.it

Texts by Andrea Minoglio
Illustrations by Bethany Lord
Translation from Italian: Antony Shugaar
Cover design, typesetting and layout: Romina Ferrari (Italian) and Ewelina Proczko (English)
Editor of original Italian edition: Francesca Pellegrino

ISBN: 978-3-03964-101-7
First edition: 2026
Printed in the Czech Republic

Mittlere Strasse 4
4056 Basel
Switzerland

HELVETIQ
helvetiq.com

FSC
www.fsc.org
MIX
Paper from responsible sources
FSC® C014138

ANDREA MINOGLIO

FASTER THAN A JET, BIGGER THAN A WHALE

An Illustrated Guide to Measuring Our World

Illustrated by
BETHANY LORD
Translated by
ANTONY SHUGAAR

TABLE OF CONTENTS

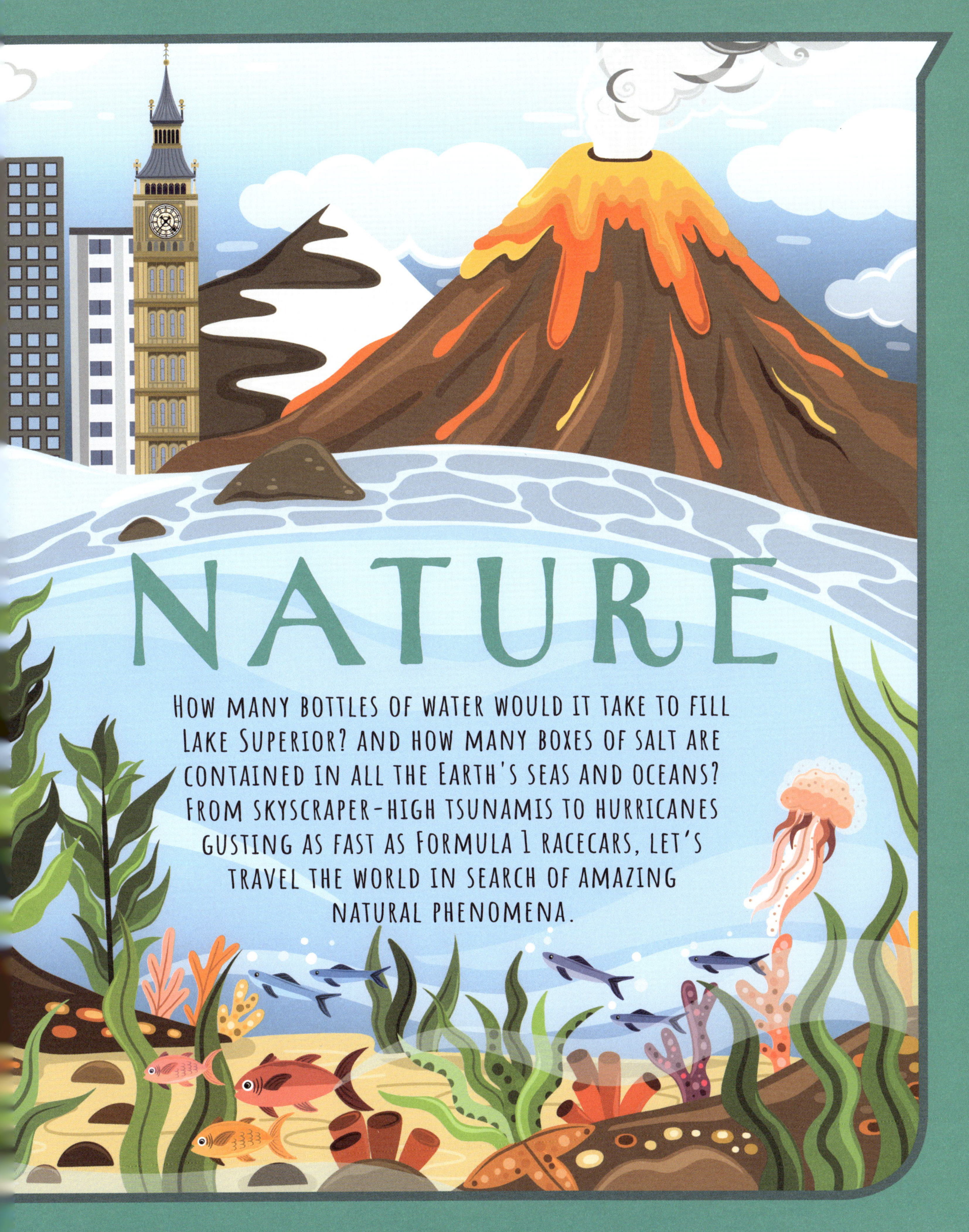

NATURE

How many bottles of water would it take to fill Lake Superior? And how many boxes of salt are contained in all the Earth's seas and oceans? From skyscraper-high tsunamis to hurricanes gusting as fast as Formula 1 racecars, let's travel the world in search of amazing natural phenomena.

RIVERS

NILE (Africa): 4,100 miles (6,650 km)

AMAZON (South America): 4,000 miles (6,400 km)

YANGTZE (China): 3,900 miles (6,300 km)

MISSISSIPPI (United States): 2,300 miles (3,770 km)

VOLGA (Europe): 2,200 miles (3,551 km)

DANUBE (Europe): 1,770 miles (2,850 km)

GANGES (India): 1,600 miles (2,525 km)

MURRAY (Australia): 1,560 miles (2,508 km)

PO (Italy): 400 miles (652 km)

TAMBORASI (Indonesia): 65 feet (20 meters)

Which river is really the longest? And the shortest?

The **Po** River, the longest river in Italy, measures 400 miles—longer than the driving distance between **Piazza del Duomo in Milan and the Colosseum in Rome**. To travel the entire **Nile**, however, you'd have to run about **58 marathons**: at 4,100 miles, it is considered the longest river in the world.

But is that really true? Some researchers argue that the **Amazon** River is actually at least 60 miles longer than the Nile. It all depends on how you measure it. The length of a river is determined by measuring from its source—where it starts—to where it ends at a sea, a lake, or another river. This isn't always easy. A river may have multiple sources, or it might end in a broad delta, making it difficult to decide which point is the farthest from the source.

For that matter, it's not even clear which river is the shortest. In Italy, if you visit Cassone, a village near Lake Garda, you'll find signs confidently informing tourists that the record-holder is right before them: the **Aril** River, 575 feet in length. But that isn't true. Both the **Tamborasi** River in Indonesia and the **Kovasselva** in Norway measure around 65 feet. They are probably the shortest, but no one is 100 percent certain.

It's no coincidence that even the Guinness World Records, after a long-standing dispute between the **Roe** River (200 feet, Montana, USA) and the **D** River (425 feet, Oregon, USA), stopped recording this type of record in 2006.

LAKES

Salt lakes and freshwater seas

The **Caspian Sea**, with its 143,000 square miles of surface area, is undoubtedly the largest lake in the world (it's roughly the **size of Japan** and **about 5 times the size of Lake Superior**), but it contains... salt water.

When it comes to fresh water, however, the largest lake—defined as a body of water entirely surrounded by land—is Lake Superior, located between Canada and the United States. It is about the size of Austria. **Lake Superior**, however, doesn't contain the most fresh water. That record belongs to **Lake Baikal** in Russia.

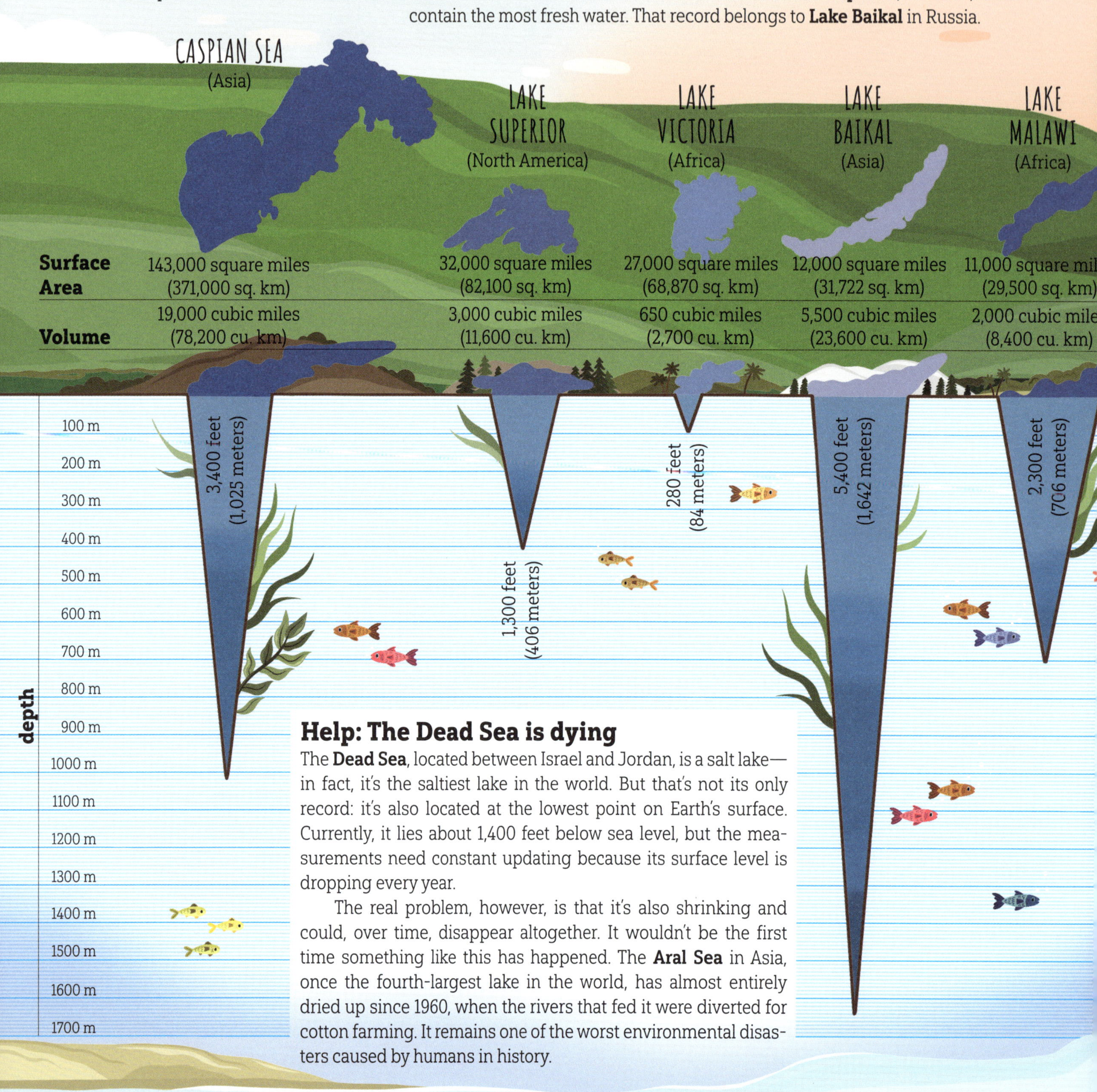

Help: The Dead Sea is dying

The **Dead Sea**, located between Israel and Jordan, is a salt lake—in fact, it's the saltiest lake in the world. But that's not its only record: it's also located at the lowest point on Earth's surface. Currently, it lies about 1,400 feet below sea level, but the measurements need constant updating because its surface level is dropping every year.

The real problem, however, is that it's also shrinking and could, over time, disappear altogether. It wouldn't be the first time something like this has happened. The **Aral Sea** in Asia, once the fourth-largest lake in the world, has almost entirely dried up since 1960, when the rivers that fed it were diverted for cotton farming. It remains one of the worst environmental disasters caused by humans in history.

Although significantly smaller in surface area than Lake Superior, Baikal is the world's deepest lake, which means it contains even more water.

But if saltwater lakes exist, could there also be freshwater seas? In a sense, yes, there could. Beneath the oceans, there are aquifers of relatively fresh water, such as the enormous one discovered by Columbia University scientists in 2019. It is located off the northeastern coast of the United States in the Atlantic Ocean. If brought to the surface, it would occupy an area nearly **half the size of Lake Superio**r, or 15,000 square miles (38,000 sq. km).

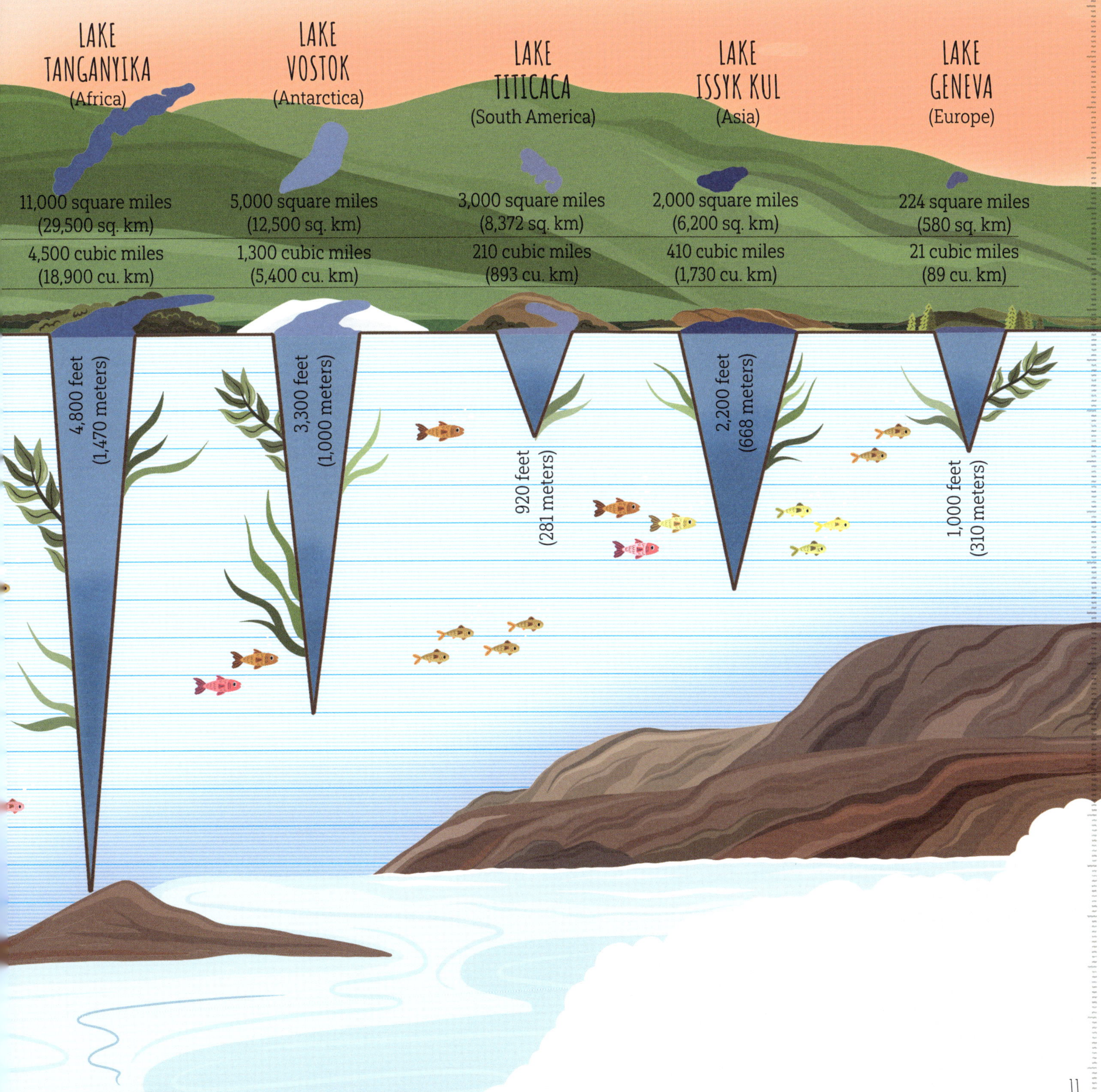

SEAS AND OCEANS

NORTH ATLANTIC

ATLANTIC OCEAN
32,870,000 square miles
(85,133,000 sq. km)
27,487 feet (8,378 meters)
Milwaukee Deep
(Puerto Rico Trench)

SOUTH ATLANTIC

Calm seas and snailfish

Since 2021, the number of oceans has officially risen to five. That is, since the National Geographic Society, after a lengthy debate, officially recognized the Southern Ocean—a vast expanse of water surrounding Antarctica—in addition to the Atlantic, Pacific, Indian, and Arctic Oceans.

But the largest ocean, in any case, remains the **Pacific**, which alone could contain every continent on Earth. The Pacific covers about **a third of the planet's surface** and holds nearly **half of all its water**. By comparison, the **Mediterranean Sea** is 54 times smaller—roughly the equivalent **of 12 bathtubs** in comparison to an Olympic swimming pool.

Speaking of which, did you know it's called the "Pacific" because, around 1520, the Portuguese explorer Magellan, after sailing across the Atlantic and navigating the strait that now bears his name (the Strait of Magellan), found it particularly calm? Over 400 years later, in 1960, near the Mariana Islands, two other explorers, Don Walsh and Jacques Piccard, descended into its depths aboard the *Trieste*, a bathyscaphe built in Italy, and for the first time reached the deepest point on Earth. Upon returning from the expedition, Piccard claimed to have seen flat fish resembling soles, but scientists believe he was mistaken. The deepest-living fish discovered so far is actually the snailfish, which is found at depths of up to "only" 5 miles.

SALTY, YES—BUT *HOW* SALTY?

Ninety-seven percent of Earth's water is salty. But have you ever wondered how much salt there is in all the seas on Earth? It can be calculated. All told, the Earth's seas contain approximately 352 quintillion gallons of water. Since each liter of seawater contains an average of 35 grams of salt, the total amount of salt in Earth's seas and oceans is roughly... 45.5 quintillion (or billion billion) kilograms. To store all that salt, you'd need **a box approximately 200 miles long (about the distance from Boston to New York City), 100 miles wide, and tall enough to reach... the International Space Station (ISS)**, which orbits the Earth at an altitude of 250 miles.

SOUTHERN OCEAN
8,480,000 square miles (21,960,000 sq. km)
4,383 feet (7,432 meters)
South Sandwich Trench

HOW MANY BOTTLES OF WATER
WOULD IT TAKE TO FILL...?

A BATHTUB
180 1-liter bottles.

AN OLYMPIC POOL
(50 x 25 x 2 meters)
2,500,000 1-liter bottles or else 13,888 bathtubs.

LAKE COMO
(5.5 cubic miles (22.5 cu. km))
22,500,000,000,000 1-liter bottles or else 9,000,000 Olympic pools.

More heat = more space

To fill an average bathtub takes about 50 gallons of cold water. But what if the water is hot? You'd need slightly less water to fill to the same level. That's because when water is heated, it expands and takes up more space. This phenomenon, called **thermal expansion**, is also responsible for about 40 percent of the rise in sea levels on Earth (the other cause being melting ice). According to NASA's measurements, sea levels are rising by about 3.4 mm per year, and over the past 100 years, they have risen an average of 17.8 cm. It might not sound like much, but it's actually significant: even a few centimeters can cause enormous damage to communities near coastlines.

What's better: a shower or a bath?

Taking a bath in a tub uses, on average, 25 to 50 gallons of water (depending on the size of the tub and how full you fill it), while a 5-minute shower consumes 10–20 gallons (depending on the type of shower).

Flushing the toilet, on the other hand, uses 1 to 3 gallons of water with each flush (depending on whether it's an older single-flush system or a modern dual-flush one). If you leave the faucet running while brushing your teeth, you waste about 2 gallons of water per minute.

If you add up all the water used for cleaning (yourself or your house), cooking, and drinking, the average household in the USA consumes around **100 gallons of water per day**.

11,600,000,000,000,000

X 515

X 323

LAKE SUPERIOR

(3,000 cubic miles (11,600 cu. km))
11,600,000,000,000,000 1-liter bottles or else 515 Lake Comos.

660,000,000,000,000,000,000

THE PACIFIC OCEAN

X 175

THE MEDITERRANEAN SEA

(900,000 cubic miles (3,750,000 cu. km))
3,750,000,000,000,000,000 1-liter bottles or else 323 Lake Superiors.

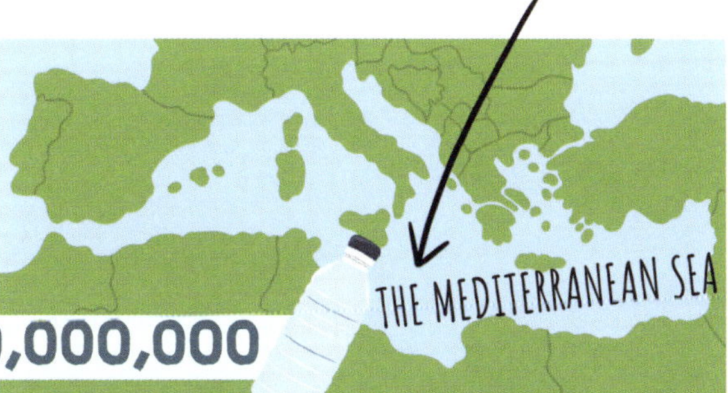

3,750,000,000,000,000,000

THE PACIFIC OCEAN

(158,000,000 cubic miles (660,000,000 cu. km))
660,000,000,000,000,000,000 (660 billion billion, i.e., quintillion) 1-liter bottles or else 175 Mediterranean Seas.

MOUNTAINS

Everest? It might not be the tallest

While many countries distinguish mountains from hills based on a specific height (e.g., above or below 2,000 feet), there's no official, universal criterion for differentiating them.

It's no coincidence that at the bottom of the list of the world's tallest mountains, you'll also find "dwarfs" like **Mount Wycheproof** in Australia, which stands just 140 feet (43 meters) tall, or **Vaalserberg** in the Netherlands, which at 1,054 feet (322 meters) represents the highest point of... the Netherlands (and there's a reason they're called the "Low Countries"!).

At the top of the ranking, however, there seems to be no doubt: **Everest** is the tallest mountain in the world! But even in this case, it all depends on how—and, more importantly, from where—you measure.

If you don't measure from sea level (diagram 1) and instead include the submerged portion of mountains (diagram 3), the **Mauna Kea** volcano on Hawaii's Big Island measures 33,497 feet (10,210 meters)—4,467 feet taller than the giant of the Himalayas! The same happens if you measure from the center of the Earth (diagram 2), which, contrary to popular belief, isn't a perfect sphere but more like a slightly squashed ball in certain places. In this case, the tallest mountain becomes Chimborazo in Ecuador, which surpasses Everest by more than 2,000 meters.

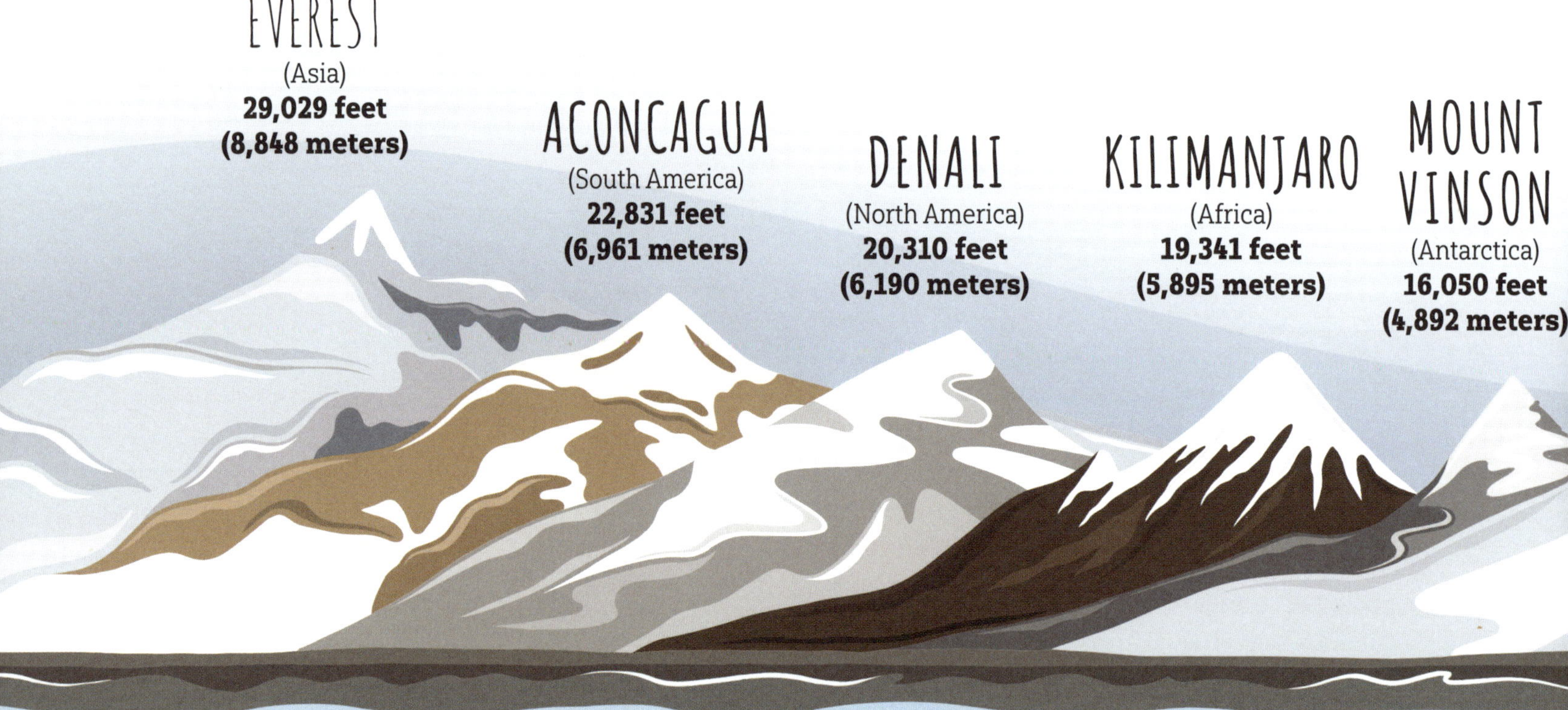

If you look beneath the sea, it's not just Everest that gets knocked off its pedestal: even the Andes become "small" compared to the mid-ocean ridge, a mountain chain running along the ocean floor. This ridge is 40,000 miles long—enough to circle the Earth one and a half times, crossing the equator along the way.

Length of mountain chains

MID-OCEAN RIDGE	40,000miles (65,000 km)
ANDES (South America)	4,300 miles (7,000 km)
GREAT ESCARPMENT (Africa)	3,000 miles (5,000 km)
ROCKY MOUNTAINS (North America)	3,000 miles (4,830 km)
TRANSANTARCTIC MOUNTAINS (Antarctica)	2,200 miles (3,500 km)
GREAT DIVIDING RANGE (Australia)	2,200 miles (3,500 km)
HIMALAYAS (Asia)	1,600 miles (2,576 km)
ATLAS (Africa)	1,600 miles (2,500 km)
ALPS (Europe)	750 miles (1,200 km)

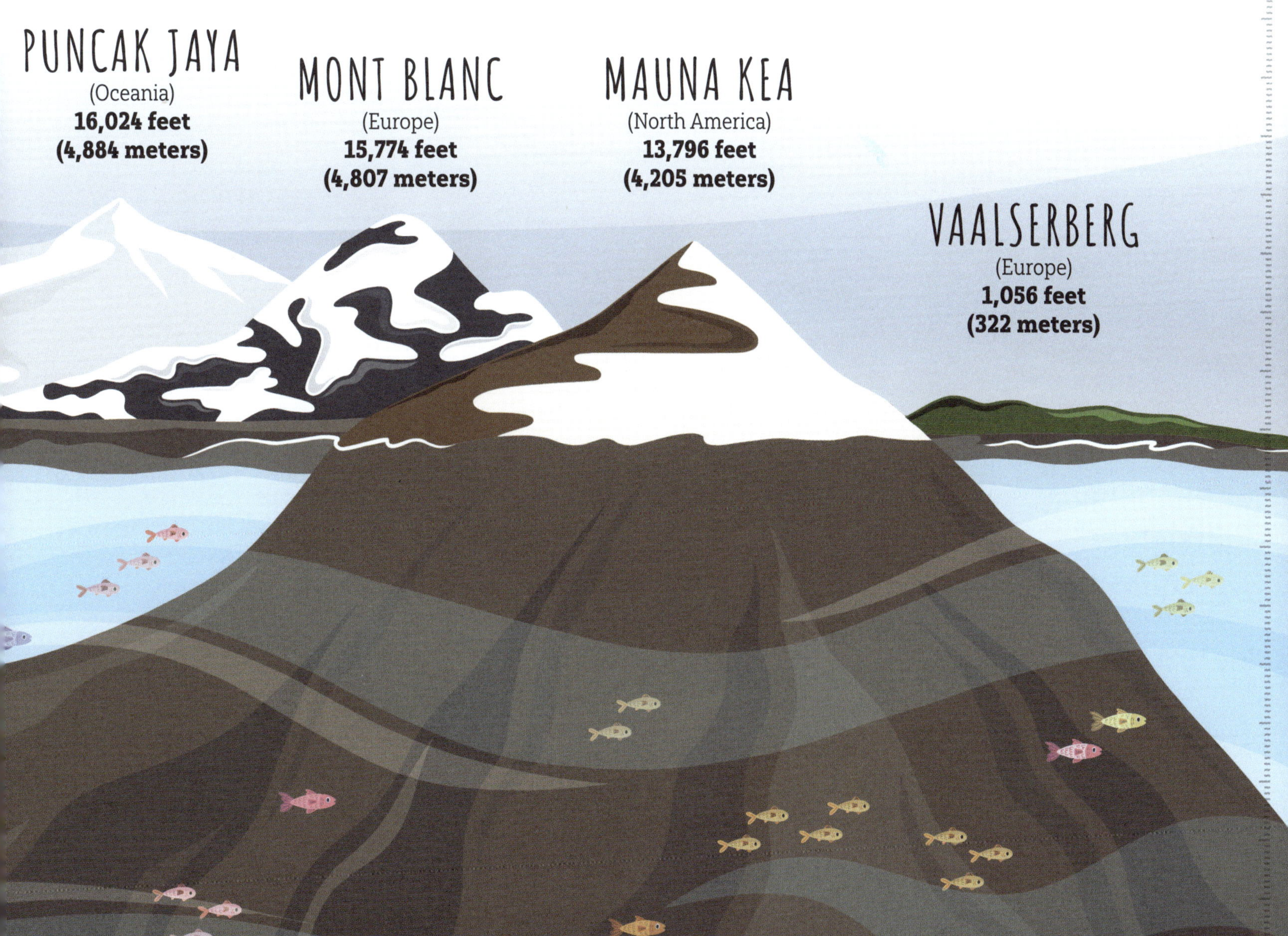

DESERTS AND FORESTS

ANTARCTIC DESERT (Antarctica)	SAHARA DESERT (Africa)	GREAT VICTORIA DESERT (Australia)	GOBI DESERT (Asia)	ATACAMA DESERT (South America)
5,483,000 sq mi (14,200,000 sq km)	3,552,000 sq mi (9,200,000 sq km)	135,000 sq mi (348,750 sq km)	500,000 sq mi (1,295,000 sq km)	54,000 sq mi (140,000 sq km)
Average annual precipitation: **6.5 in (166 mm)**	Average annual precipitation: **3 in (76 mm)**	Average annual precipitation: **9.8 in (250 mm)**	Average annual precipitation: **7.6 in (194 mm)**	Average annual precipitation: **0.6 in (15 mm)**

The sahara? It used to be all green

A desert doesn't have to be hot. One of the key considerations for calling a place a desert is the amount of precipitation (that means rain or snow, for instance...) it receives annually—less than **10 inches (250 mm) per year**. That explains why all of **Antarctica** is considered a single, vast ice desert—the largest desert on Earth. It's also home to the world's driest place, the McMurdo **Dry Valleys**, where it never rains, and what little snow does fall is swept away by powerful winds.

Among the **hot** deserts, the driest is the **Atacama Desert**, in Chile, while the largest is the **Sahara**, nearly as big **as the entire United States**. But one day, all that could become... entirely green! It wouldn't be the first time. Around **11,000 years ago**, in fact, the Sahara was full of lakes, rivers, meadows, and even forests. Then it gradually dried up due to a shift in the Earth's axial tilt—the imaginary line that our planet rotates around. That tilt changes cyclically every 20,000 years or so, affecting the climate in various regions.

AMAZON RAINFOREST
(South America)

2,031,000 sq mi
(5,260,000 sq km)

Average annual precipitation: **108 in (2,743 mm)**

CONGO RAINFOREST
(Africa)

649,000 sq mi
(1,680,000 sq km)

Average annual precipitation: **58 in (1,473 mm)**

NEW GUINEA RAINFOREST
(Oceania)

247,000 sq mi
(640,000 sq km)

Average annual precipitation: **120 in (3,000 mm)**

BORNEO RAINFORESTS
(Asia)

197,000 sq mi
(510,000 sq km)

Average annual precipitation: **79 in (2,000 mm)**

MIZORAM-MANIPUR-KACHIN RAINFORESTS
(Asia)

52,400 sq mi
(135,600 sq km)

Average annual precipitation: **79 in (2,000 mm)**

386 Trees per person

According to a 2015 study, there are about 3 trillion trees on Earth—roughly **386 per person**, based on the planet's current population. That may sound like a lot, but it's no reason to celebrate. Just 12,000 years ago, there were nearly twice as many, and we are currently losing around 15 billion trees a year—nearly one-and-a-half trees per person. To make matters worse, those trees aren't evenly distributed across the planet: only 30 percent of the Earth's land area is covered by trees. Which countries have the most trees? Canada, Russia, and Brazil.

EXTREME PHENOMENA

Earthquakes

Earthquakes are caused by sudden movements of underground rock. Their intensity can vary greatly, and scientists measure them using two main systems. The Mercalli scale classifies earthquakes on the basis of the damage they cause to people and structures, ranging from Level 1 (imperceptible) to Level 12 (apocalyptic). The Richter scale and the more commonly used moment magnitude scale (Mw) instead measure the energy released by an earthquake, known as its magnitude,

L'AQUILA
(Italy, 2009)
Magnitude 6.3

Equivalent to 42,501,898 kilograms of TNT or 2.84 Hiroshima atom bombs.

X 6.3

MESSINA
(Italy, 1908)
Magnitude 7.1

Equivalent to 673,609,687 kilograms of TNT or 45 Hiroshima atom bombs. **6.3 times more powerful than the one in L'Aquila.**

X 16

SAN FRANCISCO
(United States, 1906)
Magnitude 7.9

Equivalent to 10,675,994,076 kilograms of TNT or 712 Hiroshima atom bombs. **39.8 times more powerful than the one in L'Aquila.**

Tsunamis and megatsunamis

Some earthquakes occur in the middle of the ocean rather than on land. But even then, their effects can be devastating, as they give rise to tsunamis—massive waves that travel at high speed across the sea before crashing onto the shore. Tsunami waves can move as fast as **a passenger jet**—up to 500 mph (800 km per hour)—but they're not always towering walls of water. The waves triggered by the terrifying 2004 **Indian Ocean** earthquake (magnitude 9.2) didn't exceed 98 feet (30 meters), yet they struck multiple countries (Indonesia, Sri Lanka, Thailand...) and caused 230,000 deaths, making it the deadliest tsunami in history. In contrast, the waves formed in **Lovatnet** Lake, Norway, in 1936 were more than twice as high—but they weren't caused by an earthquake. Instead, they resulted from a massive landslide crashing into the water. When tsunamis are triggered by something external—falling rocks, landslides, meteorites—they are called "megatsunamis." The tallest one ever recorded reached a staggering 525 meters (1,722 feet)—high enough to completely submerge the Empire State Building in New York City!

INDIAN OCEAN
2004
Wave height: **100 feet (30 meters)**

TOHOKU
(Japan, 2011)
Wave height: **130 feet (40 meters)**

LOVATNET
(Norway, 1936)
Wave height: **240 feet (74 meters)**

which can range from 1 to 10. A **magnitude 1** earthquake has energy equivalent to roughly **70 lbs (32 kg) of TNT** and is imperceptible—over a million earthquakes of magnitude 1 and 2 occur worldwide every year. Earthquakes stronger than **magnitude 8** are much rarer (about one every 1–2 years), but they can cause catastrophic destruction. The 2011 earthquake in Japan, which also damaged the Fukushima nuclear plant, released more than **31,000 times** the energy of the atomic bomb that devastated Hiroshima at the end of World War II.

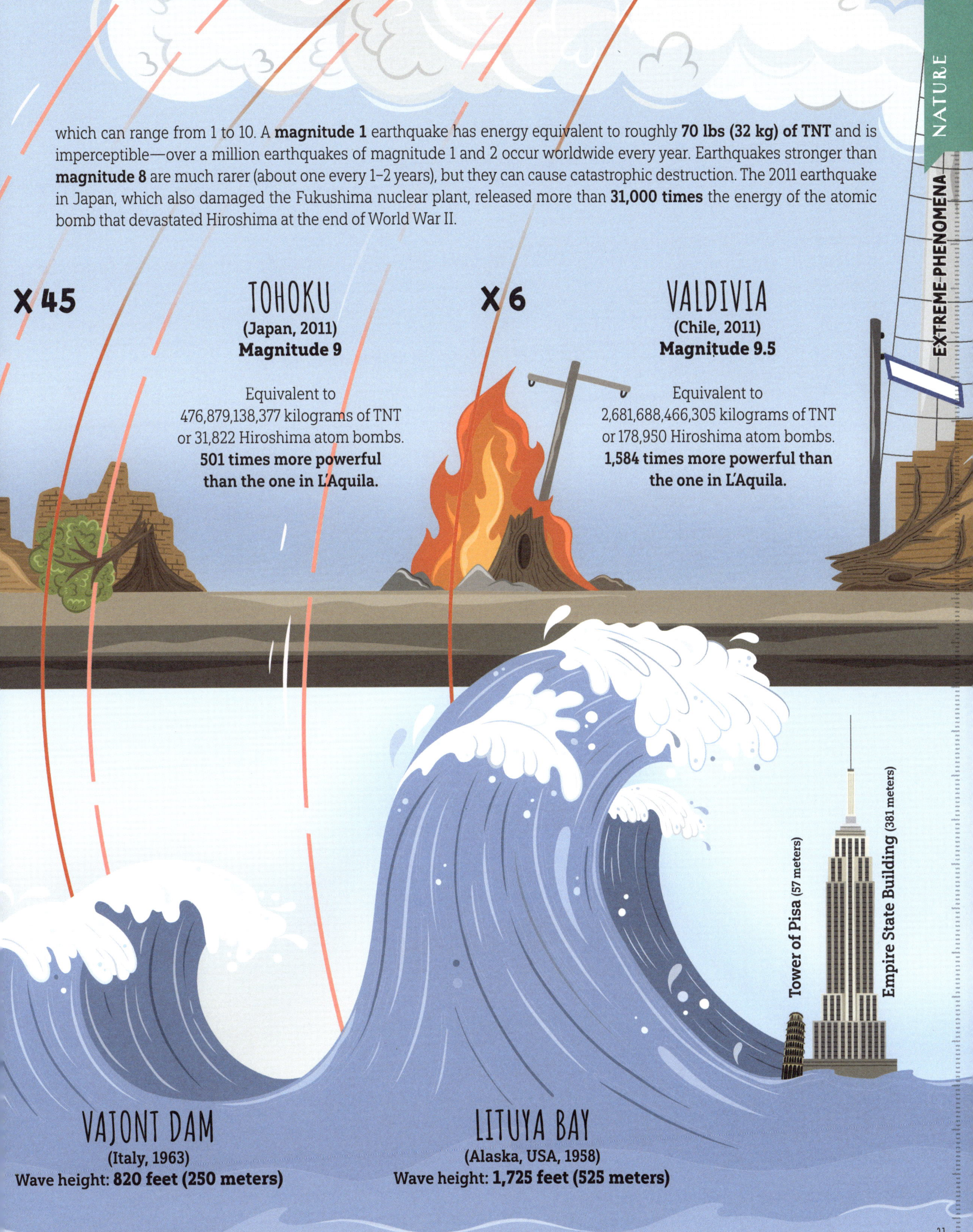

Hurricanes and typhoons

Even though they have different names, a typhoon and a hurricane are actually the same thing. Both are tropical cyclones—their name simply depends on where they form. If they develop over the Atlantic Ocean, they're called hurricanes; if they form over the Pacific Ocean, they're called typhoons. They are classified according to wind speed, which is what determines the way they move. The strongest ones—Category 5—reach speeds of over 157 mph (252 km/h), but the record is an astonishing 214 mph (345 km/h), about as fast as a **Formula 1 race car**! That record belongs to **Hurricane Patricia** (Mexico, 2015). **Typhoon Haiyan** (Philippines, 2013) was slightly slower at 196 mph (315 km/h), but it was still powerful enough to lift boulders the size of a car and weighing as much as a hippopotamus! Winds inside **tornadoes** can be even faster—over 310 mph (500 km/h)—but tornadoes are much smaller than cyclones (no more than 1.8 miles (3 km) in diameter) and usually don't travel long distances.

	MODERATE WIND	STRONG WIND	GALE	STORM
Wind velocity	**12–17 mph** **Fast as a bicycle**	**31–38 mph** **Fast as a 50 cc scooter**	**40–45 mph** **Fast as an ostrich**	**55–65 mph** **Fast as a cheetah**
Visible effects	**Dust is blown into the air.**	**Branches break.**	**Trees sway.**	**Trees are uprooted and blown away.**

Volcanic eruptions

The intensity of volcanic eruptions is classified using a scale called the Volcanic Explosivity Index (VEI), which ranges from 0 to 8 and measures the amount of material ("tephra") ejected by the volcano.

VEI 4

Material expelled >0.1 km³

CATACLYSMIC ERUPTION (VEI 4)

More than 0.1 km³ of material expelled—enough to fill **40 Great Pyramids of Giza** or **40,000 Olympic swimming pools.** Example: Eyjafjöll (Iceland, 2010)

VEI 5

Material expelled >1 km³

PAROXYSMAL ERUPTION (VEI 5)

More than 1 km³ of material expelled—enough to fill **400 Great Pyramids of Giza** or **400,000 Olympic swimming pools.** Example: Vesuvius (Italy, 79 AD)

VEI 6

Material expelled >10 km³

COLOSSAL ERUPTION (VEI 6)

More than 10 km³ of material expelled—enough to fill **4,000 Great Pyramids of Giza** or **4,000,000 Olympic swimming pools.** Example: Krakatoa (Indonesia, 1883)

THE SMALLEST
Tracy (Australia, 1974)
Diameter:
62 miles (100 km)

THE BIGGEST
Tip (Philippines, 1979)
Diameter:
1,380 miles (2,220 km)

HURRICANE
Category 1

74–95 mph

Fast as a car on the highway

Buildings and houses are destroyed.

HURRICANE
Category 5

Over 155 mph

Fast as a Formula 1 race car

Boulders the size of cars are lifted and thrown.

Over the last 132 million years, there have been about 40 eruptions at VEI 8, the highest level. One of the most significant was in the **Deccan Traps**, India, around 65 million years ago. It altered the global climate and, according to some scientists, contributed to the extinction of the dinosaurs, alongside the massive asteroid impact in Mexico that occurred around the same time. In modern history, the most powerful eruption was that of the volcano **Mount Tambora** in 1815, which triggered a global climate and economic disaster so severe that 1816 became known as "the year without a summer." To survive the resulting famine, many people resorted to eating their horses. There are even theories that this may have led to the invention of the bicycle as an alternative means of transportation.

VEI 7

Material expelled >100 km³

VEI 8

Material expelled >1,000 km³

SUPER-COLOSSAL ERUPTION **(VEI 7)**

More than 100 km³ of material expelled—enough to fill **40,000 Great Pyramids of Giza** or **40,000,000 Olympic swimming pools.** Example: Tambora (Indonesia, 1815)

MEGA-COLOSSAL ERUPTION **(VEI 8)**

More than 1,000 km³ of material expelled—enough to fill **400,000 Great Pyramids of Giza** or **400,000,000 Olympic swimming pools.** Example: Yellowstone Supervolcano (USA, 640,000 years ago)

HISTORY OF THE EARTH IN 12 HOURS

8:00 AM

CREATION OF THE EARTH

4,540,000,000 years ago
Eon: Hadean
Due to gravity, rocks and dust drifting through space that have not yet been absorbed by the Sun gradually compact to form the planets.

8:01 AM

FORMATION OF THE MOON

4,533,000,000 years ago
Eon: Hadean
Another, smaller celestial body collides with Earth. From the impact, our satellite—the Moon—is born.

9:25 AM

ORIGINS OF LIFE

4,000,000,000 years ago
Eon: Archean
The oceans form, and the first life forms appear—single-celled organisms called "prokaryotes."

10:44 AM

PHOTOSYNTHESIS AND OXYGEN

3,500,000,000 years ago
Eon: Archean
As a result of the first photosynthetic reactions, organisms in the oceans begin to release oxygen, essential for life.

1:55 PM

EUKARYOTES

2,300,000,000 years ago
Eon: Proterozoic
The atmosphere becomes increasingly rich in oxygen. More complex organisms, the eukaryotes, develop.

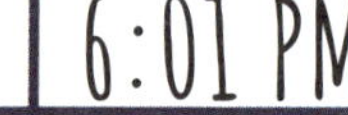

6:01 PM

SNOWBALL

750,000,000 years ago
Eon: Proterozoic
The first and longest ice age begins. Earth turns into a giant snowball.

6:34 PM

AN EXPLOSION OF LIFE

538,000,000 years ago
Eon: Phanerozoic–Era: Paleozoic
In a relatively short period, known to experts as the Cambrian Explosion, many more-complex life forms begin to spread, including vertebrates—precursors to the animals that will ultimately populate the planet.

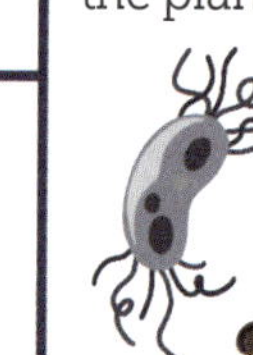

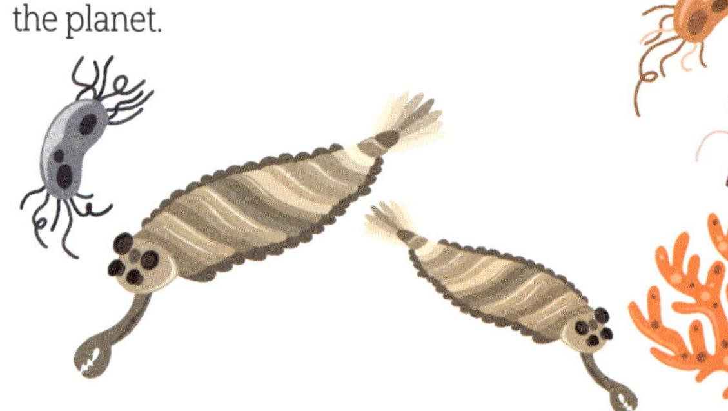

What would happen if you condensed 4.5 billion years—the age of the Earth—into just 12 hours? Just think, that's the amount of time from the moment you wake up for school to the moment you sit down for dinner. Modern humans would appear... in the last 2 seconds!

6:45 PM

PLANTS ARRIVE ON THE SCENE

470,000,000 years ago

Eon: Phanerozoic–Era: Paleozoic

The first plants begin to emerge from the water and to grow and cover the land.

6:48 PM

FIRST MASS EXTINCTION

450,000,000 years ago

Eon: Phanerozoic–Era: Paleozoic

Due to another ice age, 85 percent of marine life forms disappear.

7:20 PM

THIRD MASS EXTINCTION

250,000,000 years ago

Eon: Phanerozoic–Era: Paleozoic

Over 90 percent of life forms disappear.

7:23 PM

ERA OF THE DINOSAURS

230,000,000 years ago

Eon: Phanerozoic–Era: Paleozoic

Dinosaurs become the dominant animals on the planet.

7:31 PM

FORMATION OF THE CONTINENTS

180,000,000 years ago

Eon: Phanerozoic–Era: Mesozoic

Pangaea, a supercontinent that contained all landmasses, starts to break apart, giving rise to the continents as we know them today.

7:49 PM

FIFTH MASS EXTINCTION

65,000,000 years ago

Eon: Phanerozoic–Era: Mesozoic

A giant meteorite smashes into Earth, causing the extinction of dinosaurs and the disappearance of 2/3 of Earth's life forms.

7:50 PM

MAMMALS BEGIN TO SPREAD

60,000,000 years ago

Eon: Phanerozoic–Era: Cenozoic

Mammals diversify and become increasingly widespread, eventually becoming the dominant life forms on Earth.

7:59:02 PM

HOMININS

6,000,000 years ago

Eon: Phanerozoic–Era: Cenozoic

The first hominins, including our ancestors, evolve from an African ape.

7:59:27 PM

STONE AGE

3,400,000 years ago

Era: Cenozoic–Epoch: Pliocene/Pleistocene

The first stone tools are made.

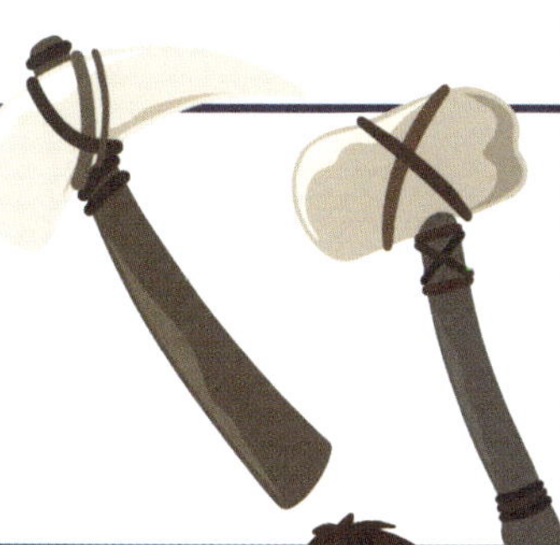

7:59:58 PM

MODERN HUMANS

200,000 years ago

Era: Cenozoic–Epoch: Pliocene/Pleistocene

Modern humans appear: *Homo sapiens.*

PLANETS

If Mars were a marble...

If **Earth** were the size of a **ping-pong ball, Jupiter** would look like a **giant Pilates fitball**, the kind people use for workouts at the gym. Though our planet may be small, it has one very special feature: its temperature. Earth is neither too hot nor too cold, which scientists believe makes it perfect for life. On **Venus**, however, it's as **hot as the inside of a wood-fired pizza oven**! Not only that—the Sun only rises every 243 Earth days! That's because a day (the time between one sunrise and the next) isn't the same on every planet. The length depends on how fast a planet rotates on its axis; it is also affected by how long it takes the planet to orbit the Sun.

JUPITER

Diameter: 88,846 miles (142,984 km)
About the size of a small fitness ball (18 inches or 45 cm)
Average temperature: -166.0°F (-110°C)
Length of a solar day:
9 hours and 55 minutes
Length of a year:
11.86 Earth years

SATURN

Diameter: 74,898 miles (120,536 km)
About the size of an inflatable beach ball (14 inches or 35 cm)
Average temperature: -220°F (-140°C)
Length of a solar day:
over 10 hours and 47 minutes
Length of a year:
29.46 Earth years

URANUS →

Diameter: 31,763 miles (51,118 km)
About the size of a handball (6 inches or 15 cm)
Average temperature: -319°F (-195°C)
Length of a solar day:
17 hours and 14 minutes
Length of a year:
84 Earth years

HOW OLD WOULD I BE ON ANOTHER PLANET?

When would I celebrate my birthday on Neptune? A year doesn't last the same on every planet—it depends on how long it takes the planet in question to complete one orbit around the Sun. On Earth, that's about 365 days. On Mars, it takes almost twice as long—687 Earth days. On Mercury, **you'd be blowing out candles and getting presents** every 3 months, since a year lasts only 88 days.

But how old would you be on other planets if you were born on February 19, 2013? On Mercury, you'd be 38 years old, on Venus, you'd be 15. On Mars, you'd now be 4 years old, while on Jupiter, Saturn, or Uranus... you'd be less than 1 year old! But on Neptune, where one year lasts 164 Earth years, your next birthday wouldn't come back around until Earth year 2177!

SUN

Diameter: 865,384 miles (1,392,700 km)
About the size of a giant ball with a 172-inch (437-cm) diameter
Core temperature: 27,000,000°F (15,000,000°C)
Surface temperature: 9,932°F (5,500°C)

NEPTUNE

Diameter: 30,775 miles (49,528 km)
About the size of a sponge ball (5.5 inches or 14 cm)
Average temperature: -328°F (-200°C)
Length of a solar day: 16 hours and 6 minutes
Length of a year: 164.79 Earth years

VENUS

Diameter: 7,521 miles (12,104 km)
About the size of a squash ball (1.5 inches or 3.9 cm)
Average temperature: 867°F (464°C)
Length of a solar day: 117 days
Length of a year: 224 days

MERCURY

Diameter: 3,032 miles (4,879 km)
About the size of a small marble (0.6 inches or 1.5 cm)
Average temperature: 332°F (167°C)
Length of a solar day: 176 days
Length of a year: 88 days

EARTH

Diameter: 7,926.2 miles (12,756 km)
About the size of a ping-pong ball (1.6 inches or 4 cm)
Average temperature: 59°F (15°C)
Length of a solar day: 24 hours
Length of a year: 365 days

MARS

Diameter: 4,220 miles (6,792 km)
About the size of a large marble (0.8 inches or 2 cm)
Average temperature: -85°F (-65°C)
Length of a solar day: 24 hours and 39 minutes
Length of a year: 687 days

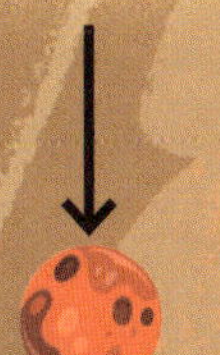

SPACE

How long would it take to get to...?

Light is the fastest thing in the universe. It travels at an incredible 186,000 miles per second (300,000 km per second)—that's seven and a half times around Earth in just one second! At that speed, reaching the moon takes just a little over one second. Unfortunately, the fastest human-made object so far—the Parker Solar Probe—traveled at a "mere" 430,000 mph (692,000 km per hour). That's less than 1 percent of the speed of light! And spacecraft designed to carry people are much slower. That's why our proposed space missions are limited, for now, to "nearby" destinations like the moon and Mars. What if we wanted to go farther, though? How long would it take? You can get an idea from the travel times listed below—or you can simply look up at the night sky, find a star, and understand that you may well be seeing it as it looked thousands of years ago—when the light you glimpse first began its journey toward us. In some cases, you might even be looking at something that no longer exists!

SUN

Distance from Earth:
94,411,000 miles (151,940,000 km)
By car: 173 years and 3 months
By plane: 17 years and 3 months
With the fastest probe:
9 days and 3 hours
At the speed of light:
8 minutes and 26 seconds

MARS

Distance from Earth:
141,952,000 miles (228,450,000 km)
By car: 260 years and 7 months
By plane: 26 years
With the fastest probe:
13 days and 18 hours
At the speed of light:
12 minutes and 42 seconds

MOON

Distance from Earth:
239,000 miles (384,400 km)
By car: 160 days
By plane: 16 days
With the fastest probe:
33 minutes and 19 seconds
At the speed of light:
1.28 seconds

HOW MUCH DO I WEIGH ON MARS?

What did the scale say the last time you stepped on it? Something like 77 lbs (35 kg)? Well, on Mars, you'd be much lighter—just 30 lbs (13 kg)! So getting around would be much easier. If you can jump 20 inches (50 cm) off the ground on Earth, you could reach a height of 35 inches (90 cm) on Mars, while on the Moon, you'd soar up about 10 feet (3 meters) off the surface! On Jupiter, however, it's a very different story. There, you'd weigh 195 lbs (88.5 kg) and struggle to hop just 8 inches (20 cm). You can blame all this on gravity, which varies from planet to planet and affects how much we weigh—and how high we can jump!

PROXIMA CENTAURI

(the star closest to the solar system)
Distance from Earth:
24,984,000,000,000 miles
(40,208,000,000,000 km)
By car: 45,868,126 years
By plane: 4,586,813 years
With the fastest probe:
6,628 years
At the speed of light:
4 years and 2 months

ANDROMEDA (the galaxy closest to Earth)

Distance from Earth: 14,914,072,571,766,814,000 miles
(24,001,873,208,937,492,000 km)
With the fastest probe:
395,674,057 years
At the speed of light:
2,535,245 years

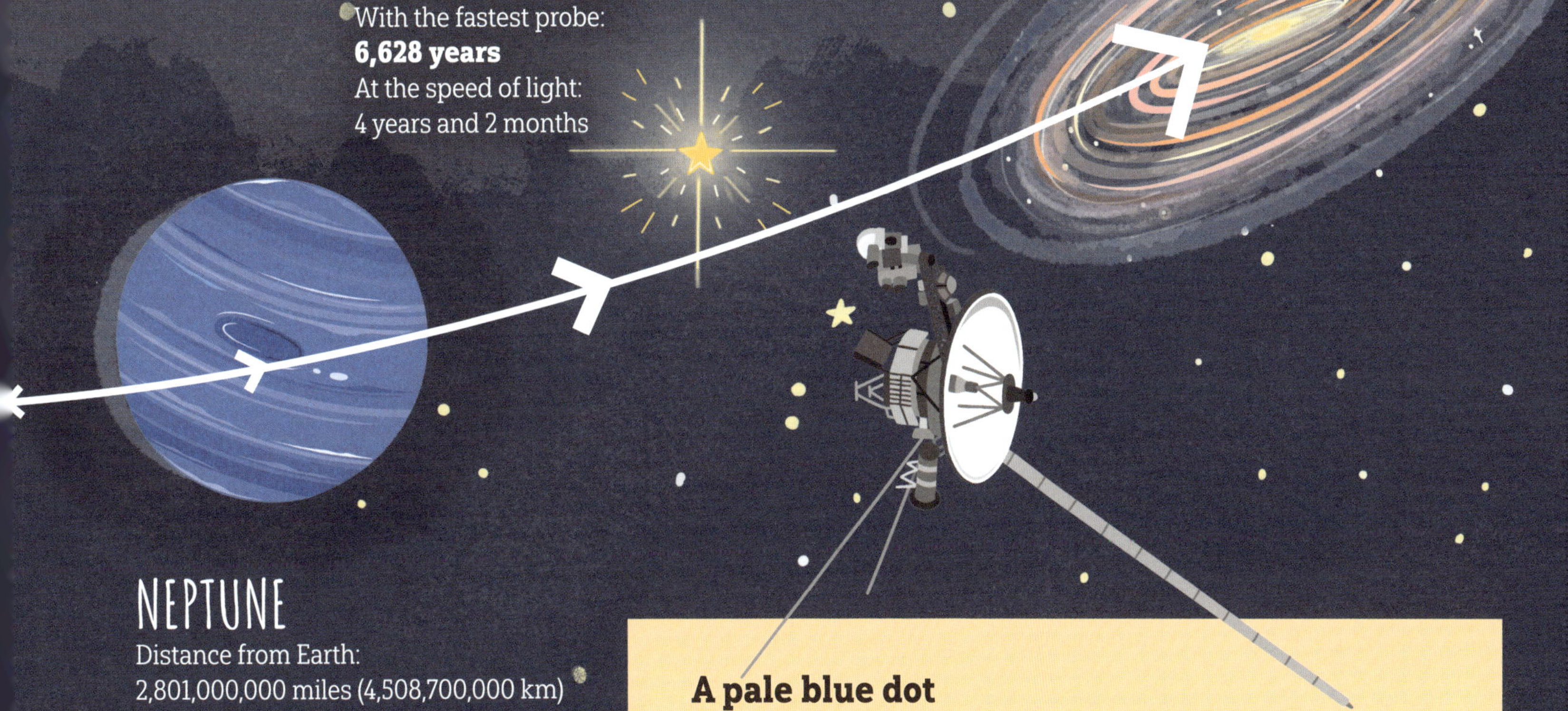

NEPTUNE

Distance from Earth:
2,801,000,000 miles (4,508,700,000 km)
By car: 5,143 years and 4 months
By plane: 514 years and 4 months
With the fastest probe:
271 days and 11 hours
At the speed of light:
4 hours and 10 minutes

A pale blue dot

The farthest distance into space ever traveled by a human-made object is more than 14 billion miles (23 billion kilometers) from Earth, by *Voyager 1*, which was launched in 1977. In 1990, when *Voyager 1* was still 3.7 billion miles (6 billion kilometers) away, astronomer **Carl Sagan** had an idea—he asked NASA to turn the spacecraft around and take a picture of Earth. He later reflected on the image with these famous words: "Our planet is a lonely speck in the great enveloping cosmic dark. In our obscurity, in all this vastness, there is no hint that help will come from elsewhere to save us from ourselves. To me, it underscores our responsibility to deal more kindly with one another, and to preserve and cherish the pale blue dot, the only home we've ever known."

LIFE ON EARTH

JUST IMAGINE SENDING ANIMALS TO THE OLYMPICS! WHO WOULD WIN IN WEIGHTLIFTING, THE GORILLA OR THE ANT? FROM TARANTULAS AS BIG AS PIZZAS TO TREES AS OLD AS THE PYRAMIDS, COMPARING ANIMALS LEADS TO SOME FASCINATING DISCOVERIES!

THE HUMAN BODY

NERVE IMPULSES

Some **nerve impulses** sent by our brain travel at speeds of up to 268 mph (432 km/h)—**faster than a Formula 1 car.**

CIRCULATORY SYSTEM

Our **circulatory system** (veins, arteries, and capillaries) measures about **62,000 miles (100,000 km)—enough to wrap around the Earth two-and-a-half times!**

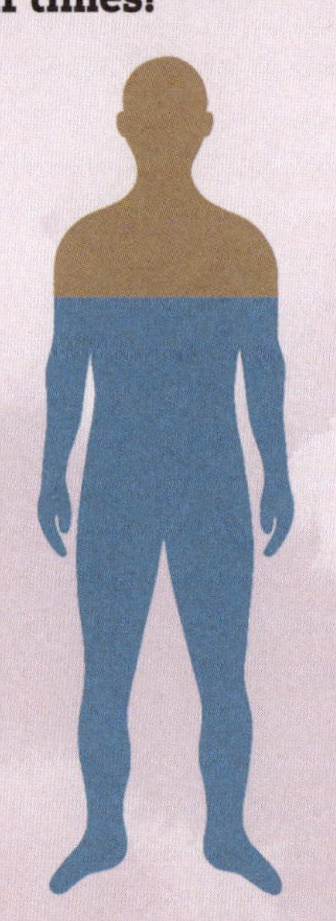

60% WATER

The human body is **60% water**—if you removed all of it, a **154-lb (70-kg) person** would weigh... about the same as an **8- to 9-year-old child**: only **62 lbs (28 kg)!**

IN 83 YEARS WE PRODUCE...

Over a lifetime (83 years on average), we produce:
250 bathtubs of urine: 11,888 gallons (45,000 liters), about 1.6 quarts (1.5 liters) per day
235 bathtubs of mucus: 11,204 gallons (42,413 liters), about 1.5 quarts (1.4 liters) per day
168 bathtubs of saliva: 8,003 gallons (30,295 liters), about 1 quart (1 liter) per day
875 bathtubs of sweat: 41,616 gallons (157,534 liters), between half a quart (half a liter) to 2.6 gallons (10 liters) per day
33 bathtubs of tears: 1,600 gallons (6,059 liters), about 0.4 pint (0.2 liters) per day

DNA

The strand of DNA inside a single cell, if unraveled, is about **6 feet (1.8 meters) long**.

If we combined the DNA from all the cells in a single human body (about 30 trillion, according to the most recent estimates), it would be long enough to travel to Neptune and back six times—**a total distance of 33 billion miles** (54 billion km)!

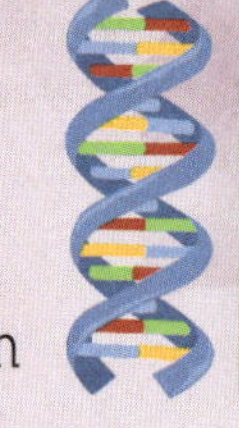

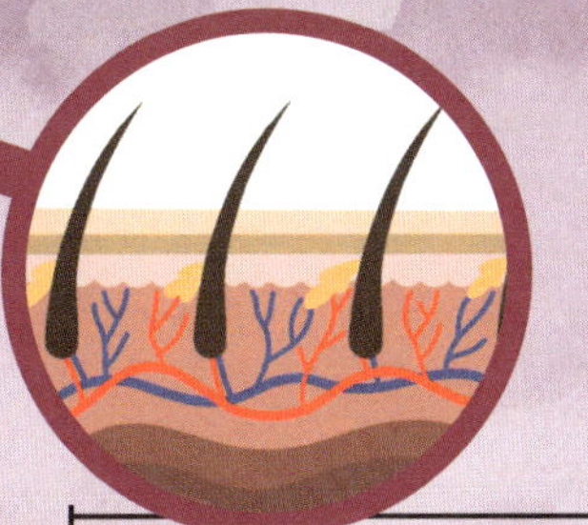

HAIR

Hair grows about **5.9 inches (15 cm)** per year, and over an average lifetime, it would reach a total length of **40.7 feet (12.4 meters).**

5.9 inches (15 cm)

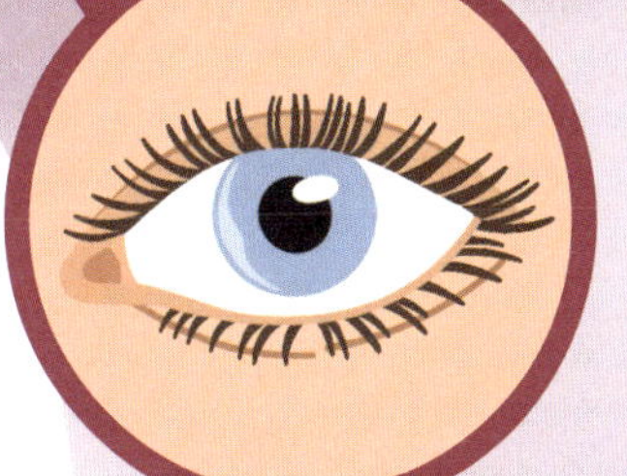

EYELIDS

Our eyelids open and close around **20,000 times per day**, about once every 3 seconds, not including sleep.

SKIN

The skin of a 154-lb (70-kg) adult weighs **22 lbs (10 kg)**, making up 15 percent of total body weight. It covers an area of **16–22 square feet (1.5–2 square meters)**—about the size of a blanket on a single bed.

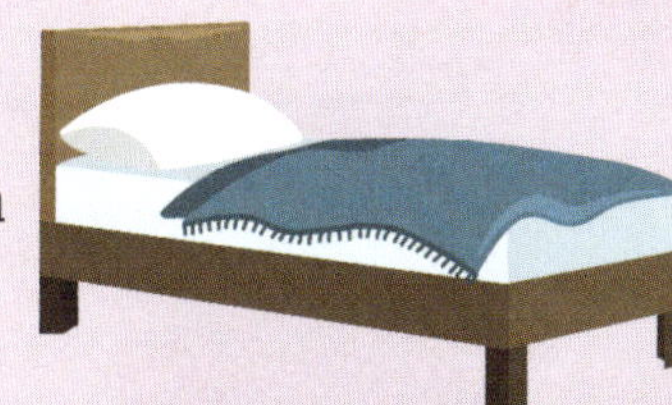

INTESTINE

The average length of the human intestine is about **26 feet (8 meters)**—longer than a soccer goal is wide. Its surface area is roughly **430 square feet (40 square meters)**—about the size of a small studio apartment or 10 ping-pong tables!

FINGERNAILS AND TOENAILS

Your nails grow about **⅛ of an inch (3.5 mm)** per month and 11 feet (3.5 meters) over a lifetime. The nails on the hand you write with grow faster, while toenails grow more slowly. However, the common myth that nails continue to grow after death is false.

⅛ of an inch (3.5 mm)

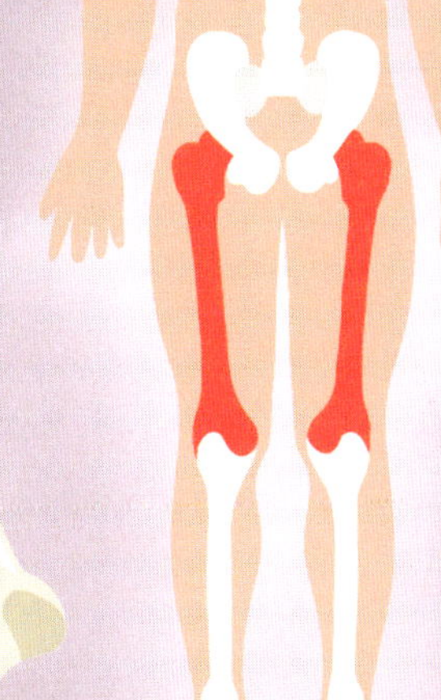

BONES

The femur is the longest bone in the human body. Found in the thigh, it typically measures about one-quarter of a person's height.

The smallest bone is the stapes (or stirrup), located inside the **ear**. It is only about 0.12 inches (3 mm) long!

GEOGRAPHY

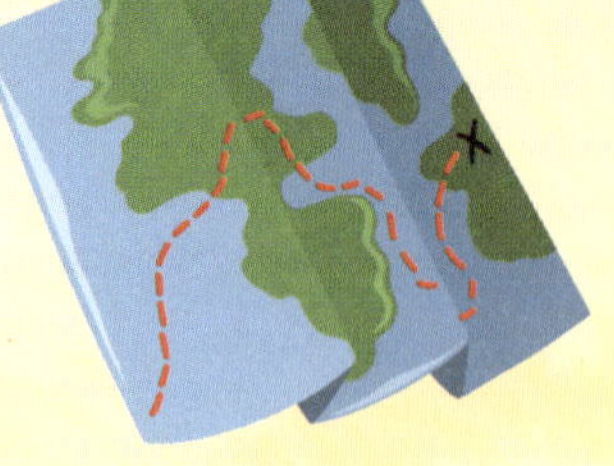

Four babies per second

Every day, about 385,000 babies are born worldwide—**more than 4 per second**! That's enough to fill **New York's MetLife Stadium (80,000 seats)** in just over 5 hours and to repopulate California and New York State (about 60 million people) in about 5 months. But where do all these people live? More than one-third of the world's population is concentrated in just two countries—**China** and **India**—which together account for over 35 percent of the planet's 8 billion people. However, having more people doesn't always mean having more space. **Russia** is the largest country in the world, covering over 12 percent of Earth's land area, but it is home to only 1.85 percent of the global population. India, on the other hand, takes up just 2 percent of the world's land but holds a staggering 17 percent of the total population!

In some places, people have plenty of space; in others, things get crowded. This depends on population density—the average number of people living in a given area. For example, the **Tokyo** metropolitan area has over 37 million residents, which is more than the **entire population of Australia,** even though Tokyo is 7,689 times smaller! And in **Macau**, the most densely populated region on Earth, about 21,000 people live in every 0.39 square miles (1 square kilometer)—as if **150 soccer players were crammed onto a single field!**

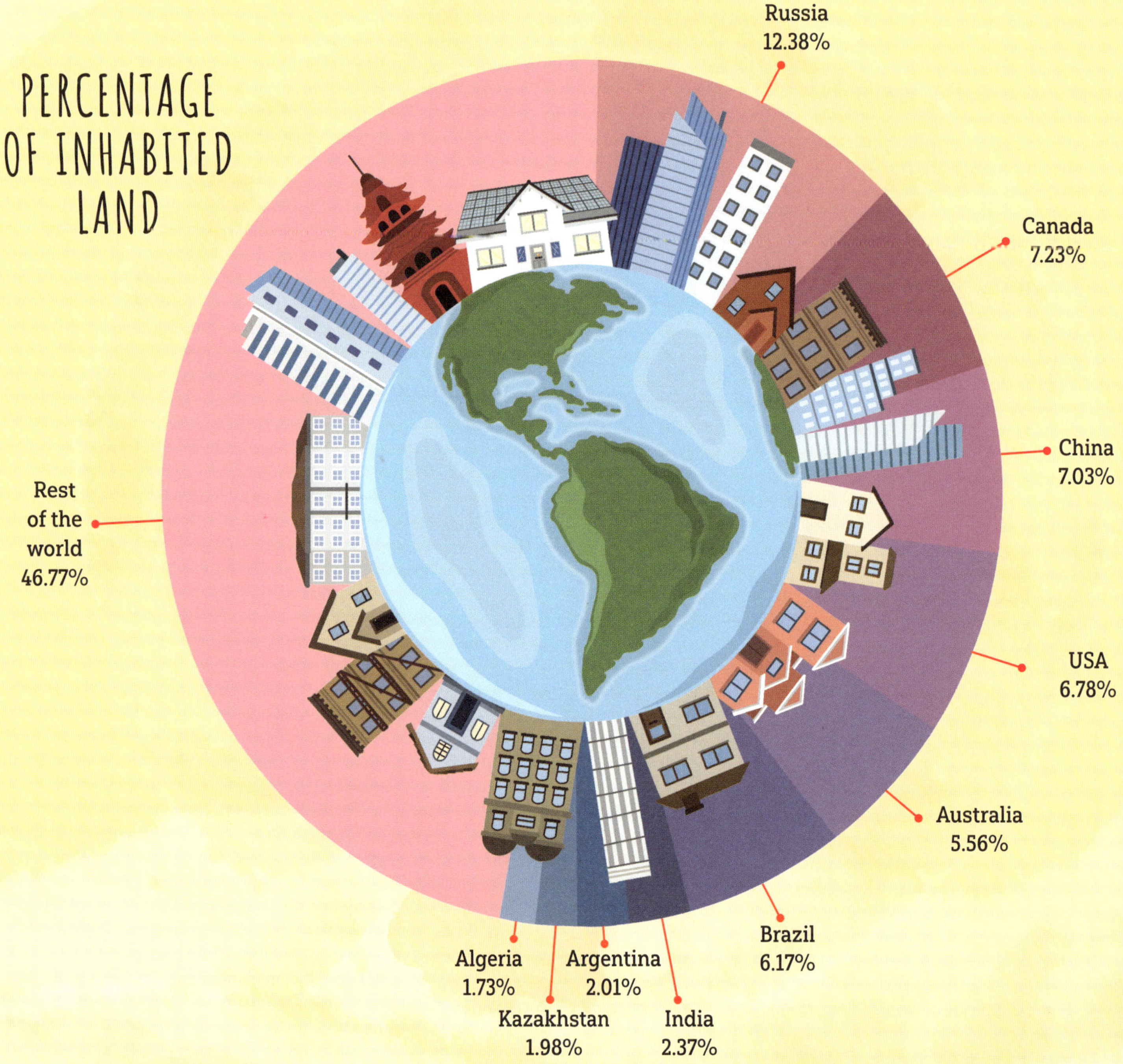

PERCENTAGE OF INHABITED LAND

Russia 12.38%

Canada 7.23%

China 7.03%

USA 6.78%

Australia 5.56%

Brazil 6.17%

India 2.37%

Argentina 2.01%

Kazakhstan 1.98%

Algeria 1.73%

Rest of the world 46.77%

To get a sense of these differences, consider **Mongolia**—one of the least densely populated places on Earth—where, on average, only 2 people live in each square kilometer (a little less than half a square mile). The least populated and smallest country in the world (in this case, the two coincide) is **Vatican City.** Its entire population—825 people—could fit on a **single airplane, like an Airbus A380-800!**

NUMBER OF INHABITANTS

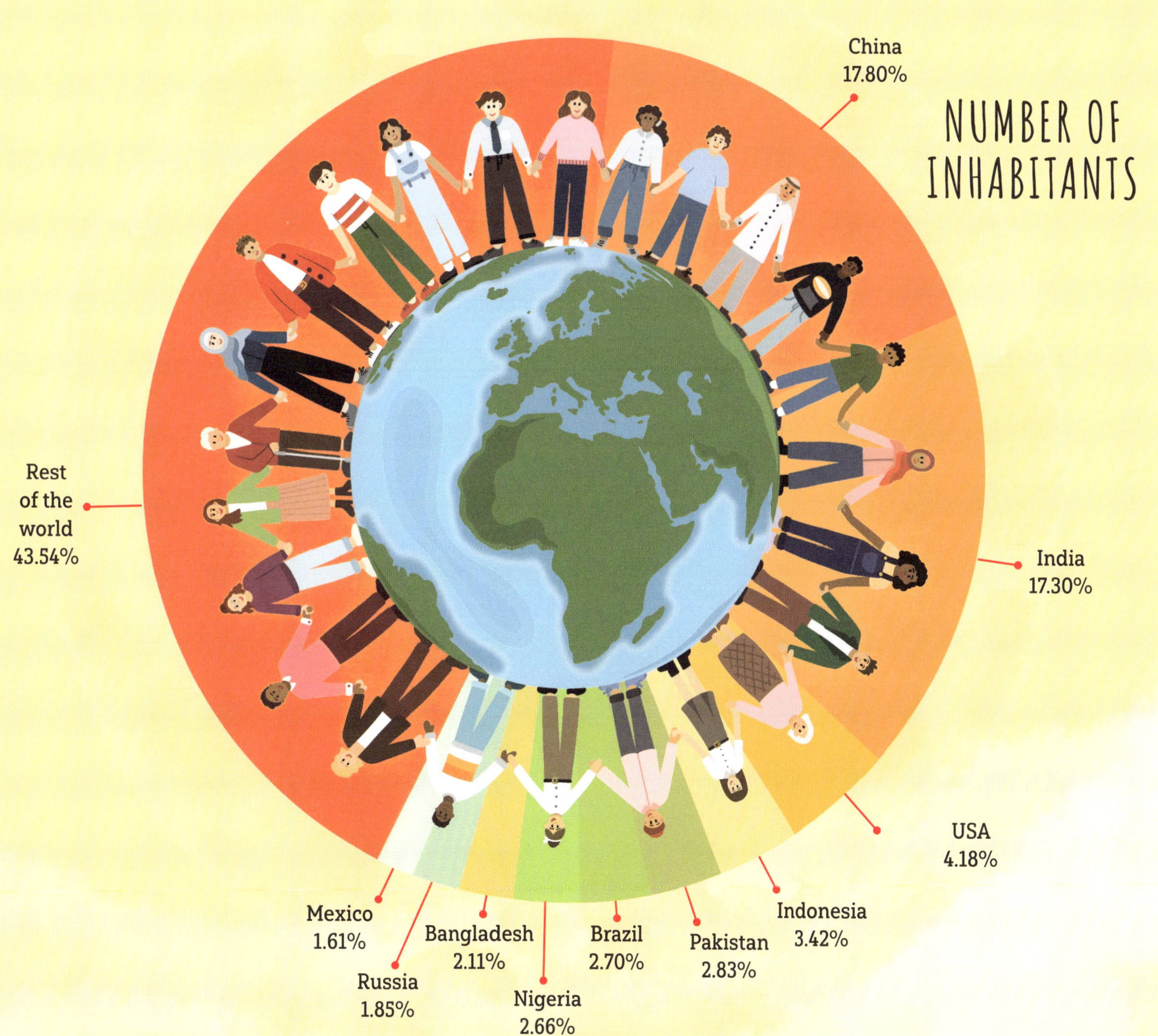

ANIMALS
SIZE AND WEIGHT

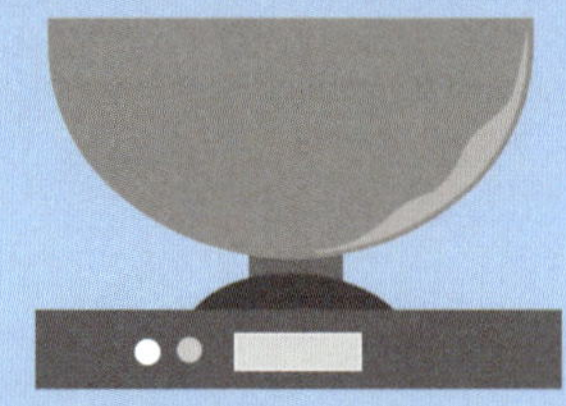

Spiders the size of pizzas and shrews as small as a USB stick

How would you react if, at dinner, you found a spider bigger than your plate and almost as heavy as a pizza? The **Goliath birdeater tarantula** (*Theraphosa blondi*) can reach 12 inches (30 cm) in size, including its legs, and weigh up to 6 ounces (170 grams). It competes for the title of largest spider with the **giant huntsman spider** (*Heteropoda maxima*), which has very long legs but a much smaller body. As for mammals, the smallest are shrews that are as **tiny as a USB stick**. That's the case with the **Etruscan shrew** (*Suncus etruscus*), which measures just 1.2–2 inches (3–5 cm) in length. It shares the title of smallest mammal with the **bumblebee bat**, which weighs only 0.2 ounces (6 grams) and has a tiny foot just 0.2 inches (6 mm) long!

At the other end of the scale, the **blue whale** is the largest animal of all. It **grows as long as a 10-story building** is tall (108 feet / 33 meters), **weighs as much as a mid-sized airliner** (about 440,000 lbs/200 metric tons), or the equivalent of **38 elephants**! It even surpasses Argentinosaurus, one of the largest dinosaurs ever to walk the Earth. And deep beneath the ocean, another giant lurks—the **giant squid**, a legendary creature with long tentacles covered in toothed, razor-sharp suckers. Scientists doubted its existence—until 2004, when it was finally photographed for the first time. Together with the **colossal squid** (*Mesonychoteuthis hamiltoni*), it holds the title of largest invertebrate on Earth. And its eyes—measuring around 10 inches (25 cm) in diameter—are bigger than those of any other animal!

BIGGEST MAMMAL
Blue whale
(*Balaenoptera musculus*)
Length: 108 feet (33 meters)

BIGGEST INVERTEBRATE
Giant squid
(*Architeuthis dux*)
Length: 43 feet (13 meters)

BIGGEST FISH
Whale shark
(*Rhincodon typus*)
Length: 43 feet (13 meters)

SMALLEST BIRD
Bee hummingbird
(*Mellisuga helenae*)
Length: About 2 inches (5–6 cm)

REAL 100% SIZE

SMALLEST MAMMAL
Bumblebee bat
(*Craseonycteris thonglongyai*)
Length: 1.2 inches (3 cm)

LARGEST LAND MAMMAL

African bush elephant
(*Loxodonta africana*)
Height: **10–13 feet (3.2–4 meters)**
Length: **23 feet (7 meters)**

BIGGEST BIRD

Ostrich
(*Struthio camelus*)
Height: **almost 9 feet (2.7 meters)**

BIGGEST SPIDER

Goliath birdeater spider
(*Theraphosa blondi*)
Length: **about a foot (30 cm),** including legs

The eye of the **giant squid:**
10 inches (25 cm) across

HOW MANY VERTEBRAE ARE THERE IN A GIRAFFE'S NECK?

With a height of 19.4 feet (5.9 meters), the giraffe (*Giraffa camelopardalis*) is the tallest animal on the planet. Its impressive height is mainly thanks to its long neck, which allows it to reach and feed on acacia leaves. A question naturally arises: How many vertebrae does a giraffe's neck contain? Surprisingly, it has only 7 vertebrae—the same number as a mouse, a human, and almost all other mammals! The only exceptions are sloths, which have anywhere from 5 to 9 vertebrae. Birds, on the other hand, have many more vertebrae. Swans, for example, can have up to 25!

SPEED

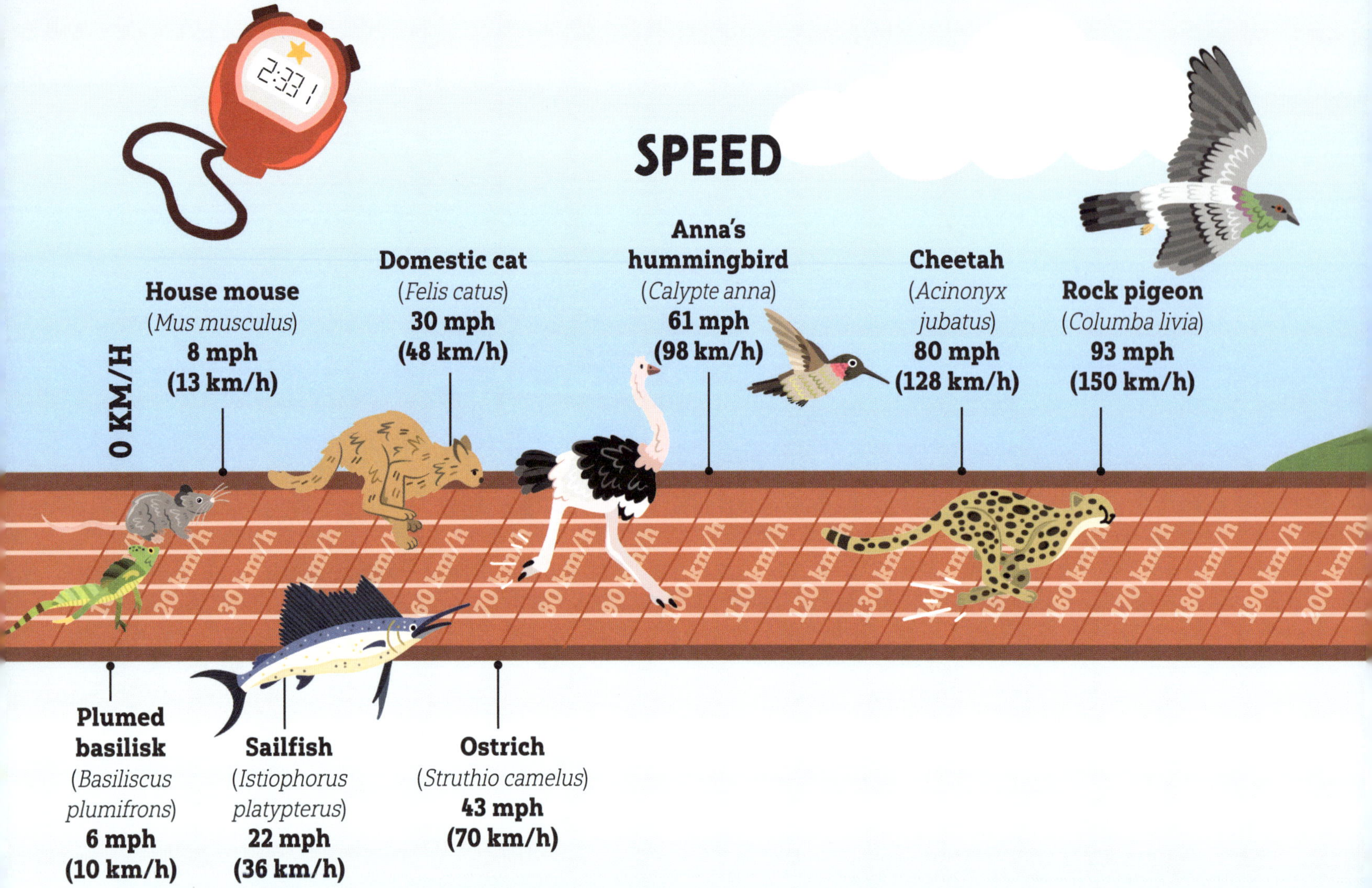

0 KM/H

House mouse
(*Mus musculus*)
8 mph
(13 km/h)

Domestic cat
(*Felis catus*)
30 mph
(48 km/h)

Anna's hummingbird
(*Calypte anna*)
61 mph
(98 km/h)

Cheetah
(*Acinonyx jubatus*)
80 mph
(128 km/h)

Rock pigeon
(*Columba livia*)
93 mph
(150 km/h)

Plumed basilisk
(*Basiliscus plumifrons*)
6 mph
(10 km/h)

Sailfish
(*Istiophorus platypterus*)
22 mph
(36 km/h)

Ostrich
(*Struthio camelus*)
43 mph
(70 km/h)

Running on water and the fastest eater

In legends, the **plumed basilisk** is a mythical creature that can kill with a single glance. In reality, however... it walks on water! When startled, it makes its escape by rapidly pumping its hind legs, reaching speeds of up to 10 km/h (6.2 mph). Scientists have calculated that for a human to pull off the same trick, we would need to run at an astonishing 100 km/h (62 mph)! When talking about speed, it's important to consider body size and weight—what's fast for one species might not be for another.

Take **Anna's hummingbird**, for example. To impress females, the male dives at 60 mph (96 km/h), covering 385 times its own body length per second—far more than the **peregrine falcon**, which is officially the fastest animal on Earth. In relative terms, Anna's hummingbird is **nearly twice as fast as a space capsule** re-entering Earth's atmosphere! Think about this: in one second, its wings beat 90 times, and its heart beats 20 times!

Remaining on solid ground, the **cheetah** holds the land record, running **three times faster than Usain Bolt**, the fastest human in the world, who reaches about 27 mph (44 km/h).

But when it comes to eating, nothing is faster than the star-nosed mole (*Condylura cristata*). This nearly blind animal has an incredible sense of touch thanks to the pink tentacle-like appendages around its nose. According to studies, it can detect whether prey is edible in just 8 milliseconds and devour it in 120 milliseconds—about ten times faster than the blink of an eye! That makes it one of the fastest eaters in the world!

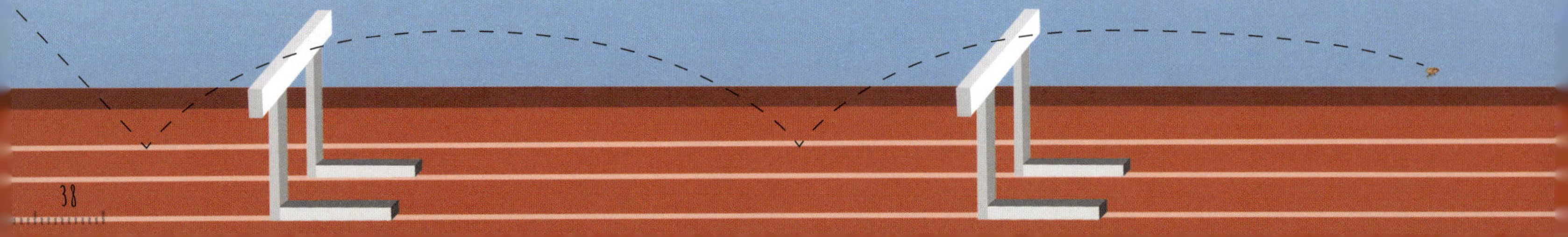

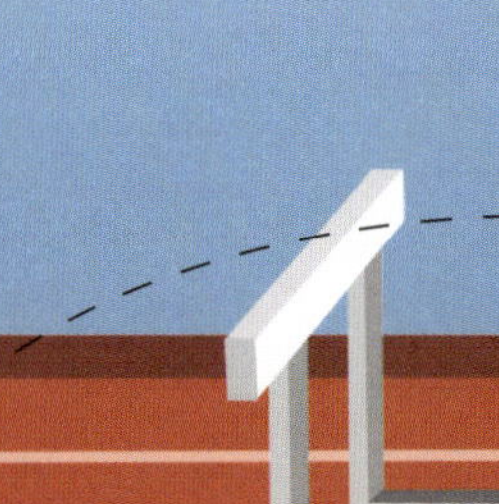

HIGH JUMP

Also known as a cougar or mountain lion, the **puma** (*Puma concolor*), widely distributed across the Americas, holds the title of world champion in high jump. With a single leap, it can reach 17.7 feet (5.4 meters)—**more than twice the height of a volleyball net**.

However, if we look at things proportionally, the **meadow froghopper** or **meadow spittlebug** (*Philaenus spumarius*) does even better. This tiny insect can jump 28 inches (70 cm)—about 115 times the length of its own body. That would be like a human jumping over a building **more than 650 feet (200 meters) tall!**

LONG JUMP

The **red kangaroo** (*Osphranter rufus*) can move at speeds of 30 mph (50 km/h), covering distances of 6 to 30 feet (2 to 9 meters) per leap. The world record for a long jump, however, belongs to the **snow leopard** (*Panthera uncia*), which has been observed leaping an incredible 50 feet (15 meters)—**the length of an entire bus**! But if we take proportion into account, the **cat flea** (*Ctenocephalides felis*) beats them all. It can jump 19 inches (48 cm)—160 times the length of its own body. For a human to match that, they would have to jump **over 3 soccer fields in a single leap**, covering a distance of 1,000 feet (300 meters)!

UP, DOWN, AND ALL AROUND THE WORLD

Freediving champions and mountain-climbing spiders

In a swimming pool in 2021, Budimir Šobat, a 56-year-old man, held his breath for an astonishing 24 minutes and 37 seconds—but only after breathing pure oxygen beforehand to prepare for the attempt. Without that special preparation, the record belongs to Stéphane Mifsud, who managed to stay underwater for 11 minutes and 35 seconds on a single breath. Impressive? Maybe—but they both pale in comparison to the ziphius, or Cuvier's beaked whale (*Ziphius cavirostris*), a marine mammal that has been recorded diving to depths of nearly 10,000 feet (3,000 meters)—**as if stepping into an elevator and going down 1,000 floors!** Even more incredible, it can hold its breath for 3 hours and 42 minutes, making it the undisputed world champion of breath-holding and deep diving! (Sea turtles can last over 6 hours without breathing, but only when they're asleep.) The deepest-diving human, using only fins and no oxygen tanks, has reached just 430 feet (131 meters). But in the abyssal depths of the ocean, many other creatures live even deeper. The record for the deepest-living fish goes to the **snailfish**, spotted at an astounding 26,000 feet (8,000 meters) in the Mariana Trench!

At the other extreme, no animal soars higher than **Rüppell's griffon** vulture (Gyps rueppelli), which can fly to altitudes over 36,000 feet (11,000 meters)—higher than most commercial airplanes! And what about spiders? In the Himalayas, there's a species of **jumping spider** that lives at extreme altitudes. However, the highest-altitude land animal ever recorded is a tiny rodent spotted by researchers in Chile at 22,110 feet (6,739 meters)!

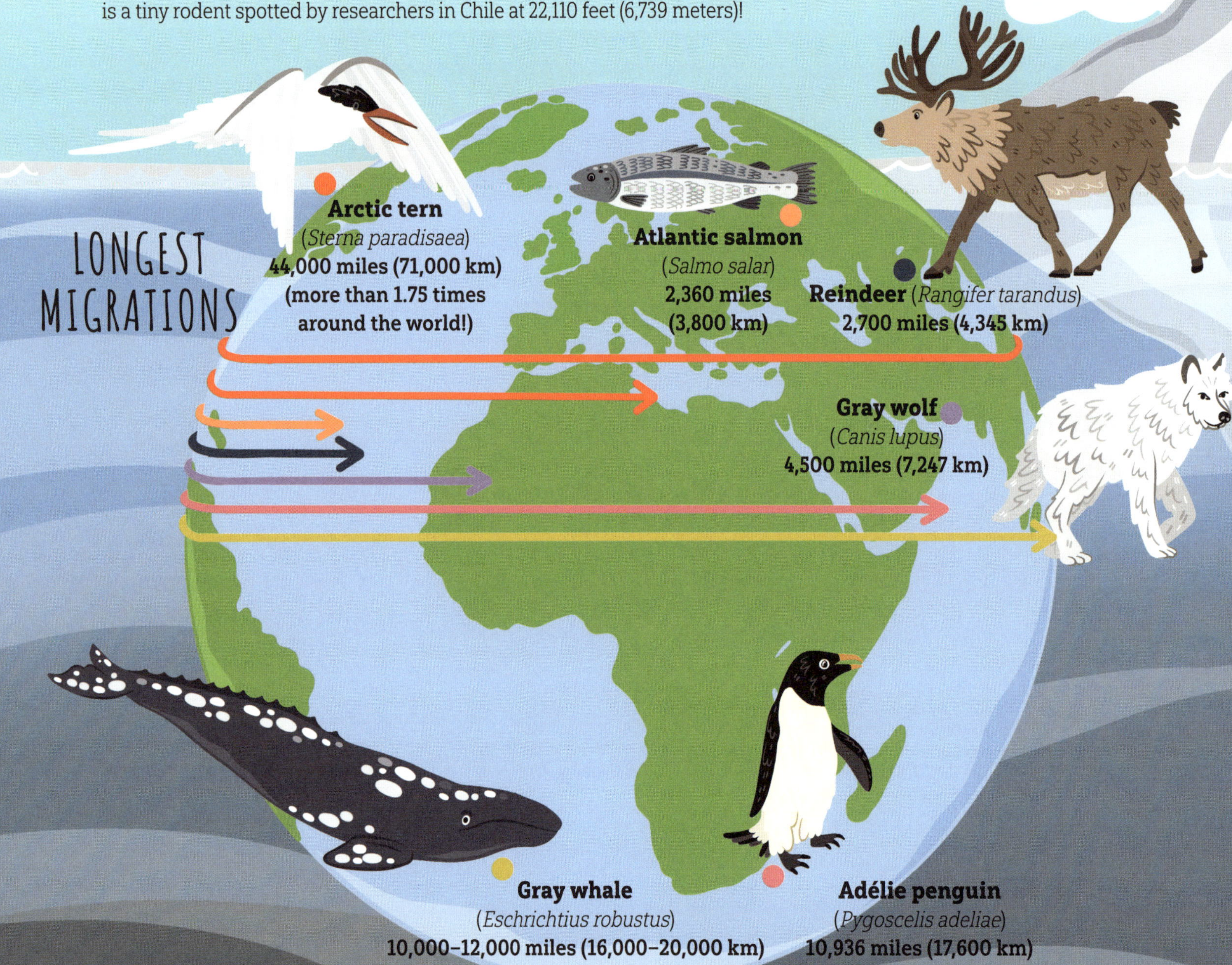

Rüppell's griffon vulture
(*Gyps rueppelli*)
36,700 feet (11,200 meters)

Bumblebee
(*Bombus*)
29,530 feet
(9,000 meters)

Whooper swan
(*Cygnus cygnus*)
27,000 feet (8,230 meters)

Himalayan jumping spider
(*Euophrys omnisuperstes*)
22,000 feet (6,700 meters)

Andean rock mouse
(*Phyllotis xanthopygus rupestris*)
22,000 feet
(6,739 meters)

Brown bear
(*Ursus arctos*)
16,400 feet (5,000 meters)

Alpine marmot
(*Marmota marmota*)
10,500 feet (3,200 meters)

9000 m
8000 m
7000 m
6000 m
5000 m
4000 m
3000 m
2000 m
1000 m

DEPTH

0 mt

HEIGHT

1000 m
2000 m
3000 m
4000 m
5000 m
6000 m
7000 m
8000 m
9000 m

Emperor penguin
(*Aptenodytes forsteri*)
1,900 feet (565 meters)
Can dive for 22 minutes

Leatherback sea turtle
(*Dermochelys coriacea*)
4,200 feet (1,280 meters)
Can dive for 86.5 minutes

Ziphius, or Cuvier's beaked whale
(*Ziphius cavirostris*)
9,816 feet (2,992 meters)
Can dive for 222 minutes

Dumbo octopus
(*Opisthoteuthis californiana*)
13,000 feet
(4,000 meters)

Snailfish
(*Pseudoliparis swirei*)
26,000 feet
(8,000 meters)

CHAMPION WEIGHTLIFTERS

HARPY EAGLE

(*Harpia harpyja*)
Can lift **its own weight.**

LEAFCUTTER ANT

(*Atta Fabricius*)
Can lift as much as **20 times** its own weight.

HUMAN BEING

(*Homo sapiens*)
Can lift **1.5 times** its own weight.

EUROPEAN RHINOCEROS BEETLE

(*Oryctes nasicornis*)
Can lift up to **100 times** its own weight.

GORILLA

(*Gorilla gorilla*)
Can lift up to **3.5 times** its own weight.

TAURUS SCARAB

(*Onthophagus taurus*)
Can lift up to **1,000 times** its own weight.

An ant? Proportionally, it lifts a hippo!

Which is stronger—a human or an ant? That depends. Georgian weightlifter Lasha Talakhadze, who holds the Olympic record, can lift 589 lbs (267 kg) in the clean and jerk category—about 1.5 times his body weight (403 lbs / 183 kg). But some **ants**, using their powerful jaws and incredibly strong neck muscles, can lift objects—like leaves—weighing up to 20 times their own body weight! That would be like a human carrying a **3,100-lb (1,400-kg) hippopotamus** or a **mid-sized car**—with their bare hands! And some rhinoceros beetles, like the **Hercules beetle**, take it even further—they can lift 100 times their body weight (though they can barely move afterward). That would be like a person hoisting a full-grown **rhinoceros... plus an elephant!** But **dung beetles are the true champions**. To match their strength, a human would have to push an airplane as heavy as a fully fueled Airbus A320! These tiny insects can roll giant dung balls amounting to 1,000 times their own body weight—an incredible feat of strength. When it comes to punching power, no human boxer stands a chance against the **peacock mantis shrimp** (*Odontodactylus scyllarus*). This aggressive crustacean throws punches at speeds of 50 mph (80 km/h)—**so powerful that they can shatter aquarium glass!**

CHAMPIONS OF ENDURANCE

The wood frog can survive temperatures as low as -4.0°F (-20°C)—**about as cold as your household freezer!** It does this by freezing nearly half of its body—its heart almost stops beating, and its breathing comes to a halt.

Emperor penguins, on the other hand, use a different technique. In addition to their thick feathers, a 1.2-inch (3-cm) layer of fat, and uniquely adapted blood, they huddle together in massive groups, forming a giant penguin hug to share warmth and thereby endure temperatures as low as -76.0°F (-60°C). Still, none of this compares to the **tardigrade**—a microscopic creature that can withstand -454°F (-270°C), close to absolute zero, the lowest temperature theoretically possible. And it's not just the cold! This 1.5 mm creature can also survive extreme heat up to 302°F (150°C), go without water for 10 years, and even survive in space, without air, for 10 days!

DINOSAURS

The largest predator? It swam—and it wasn't T-Rex

Dinosaurs came in all shapes and sizes: Armored dinosaurs (Thyreophora), like Stegosaurus and Ankylosaurus; thick-skulled dinosaurs (Pachycephalosauria), like Pachycephalosaurus; horned dinosaurs (Ceratopsians), like Triceratops; predators (Theropods), like the notorious Tyrannosaurus rex... But when it came to sheer size, nothing beat the Sauropods (those long-necked, long-tailed giants) and, especially, the largest of them all: **Argentinosaurus**. This colossal dinosaur grew to be longer than **three buses in a row**—121 feet (37 meters)—and weigh as much as **20 African bush elephants**—220,000 lbs (100 metric tons)! At least, that's what the latest estimates by paleontologists tell us. In this field, however, new fossil discoveries and advanced research are constantly changing the numbers—and with them, the way we imagine dinosaurs!

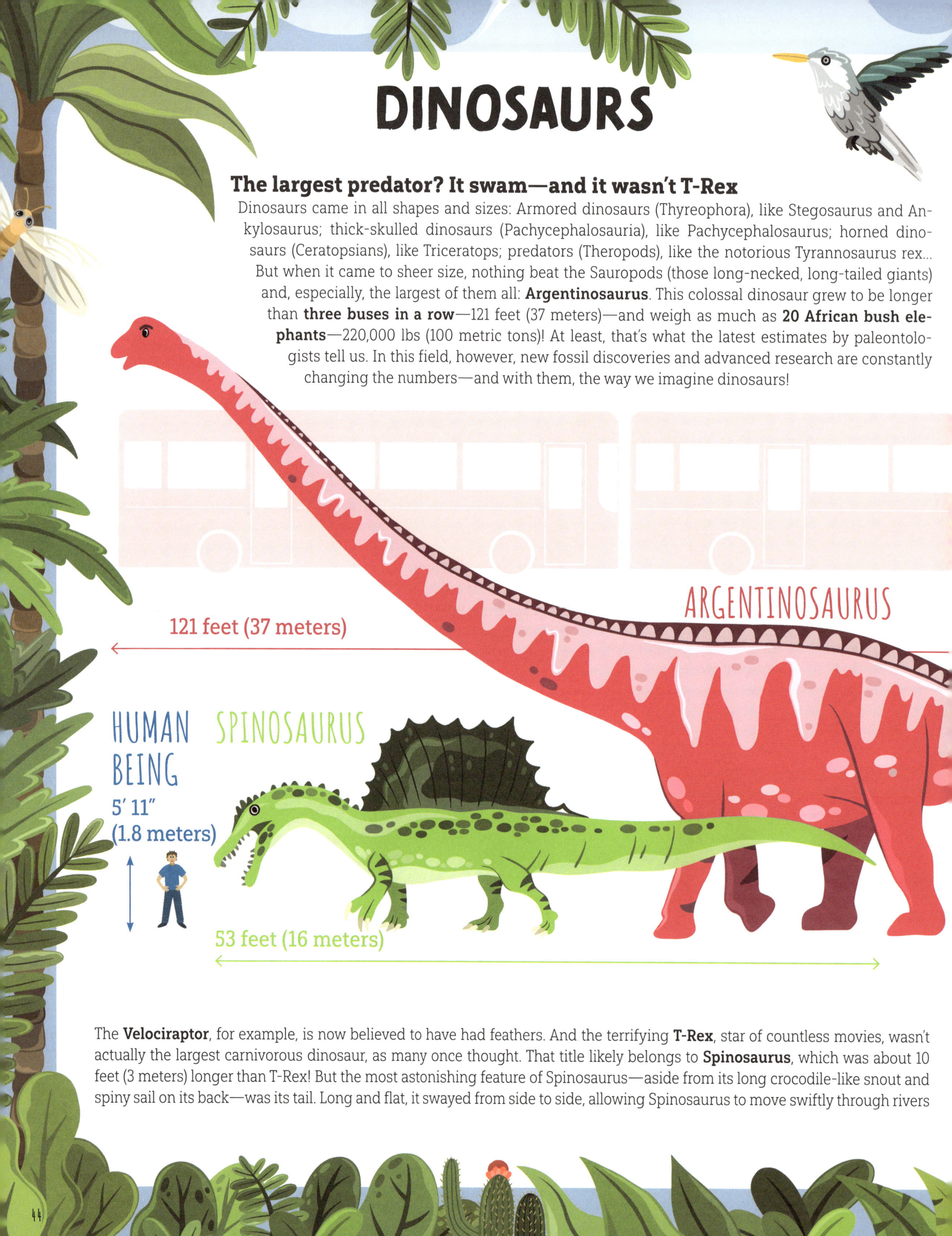

The **Velociraptor**, for example, is now believed to have had feathers. And the terrifying **T-Rex**, star of countless movies, wasn't actually the largest carnivorous dinosaur, as many once thought. That title likely belongs to **Spinosaurus**, which was about 10 feet (3 meters) longer than T-Rex! But the most astonishing feature of Spinosaurus—aside from its long crocodile-like snout and spiny sail on its back—was its tail. Long and flat, it swayed from side to side, allowing Spinosaurus to move swiftly through rivers

AND THE SMALLEST?

If Argentinosaurus was the largest dinosaur, which was the smallest? For a long time, the record belonged to *Compsognathus longipes*, which measured little more than 3 feet (1 meter) in length—**about the size of a turkey**. However, even smaller dinosaurs have been discovered, such as *Parvicursor remotus*, which was about 15 inches (40 cm) long.

Then, in 2020, paleontologists unearthed the fossil of an animal about the size of a bee hummingbird, with a skull only 0.6 inches (1.4 cm) long. At first, they thought it was the smallest dinosaur ever found—**Oculudentavis**. Later studies, however, suggested that it was actually a lizard, not a dinosaur. But the reference to the bee hummingbird wasn't entirely wrong. We now know that birds are, in fact, living dinosaurs—the ones that survived the mass extinction 65 million years ago and evolved into the species we see today. So, by that logic, the smallest bird in the world could also be considered the smallest dinosaur!

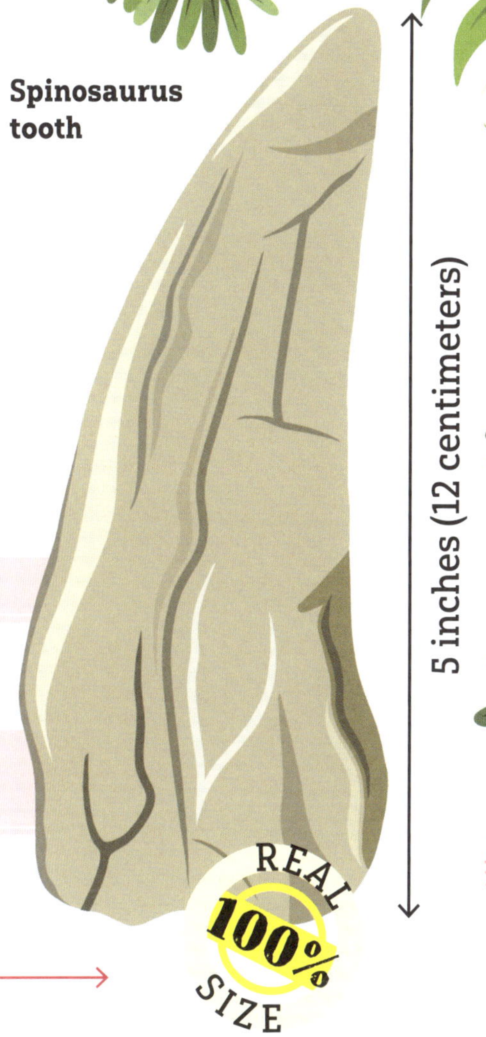

Spinosaurus tooth

5 inches (12 centimeters)

REAL 100% SIZE

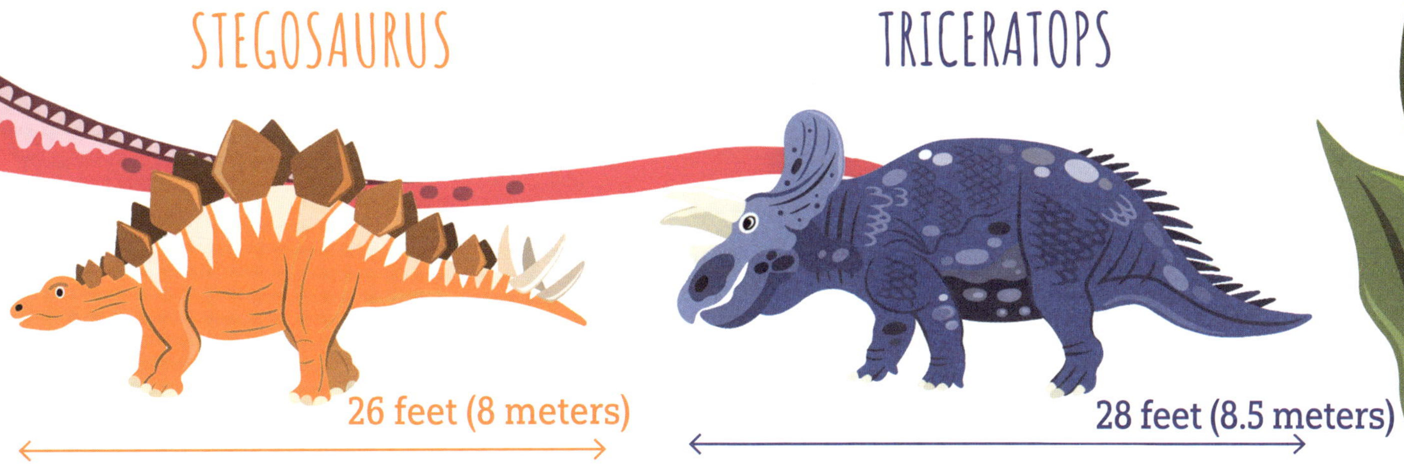

STEGOSAURUS

26 feet (8 meters)

TRICERATOPS

28 feet (8.5 meters)

while hunting prey. And those teeth? Each tooth was as long as a pencil—about 5 inches (12 cm)! According to scientists who've studied it, this is strong evidence that non-feathered dinosaurs eventually invaded aquatic environments, rather than remaining only on land.

TREES, FLOWERS, AND FUNGI

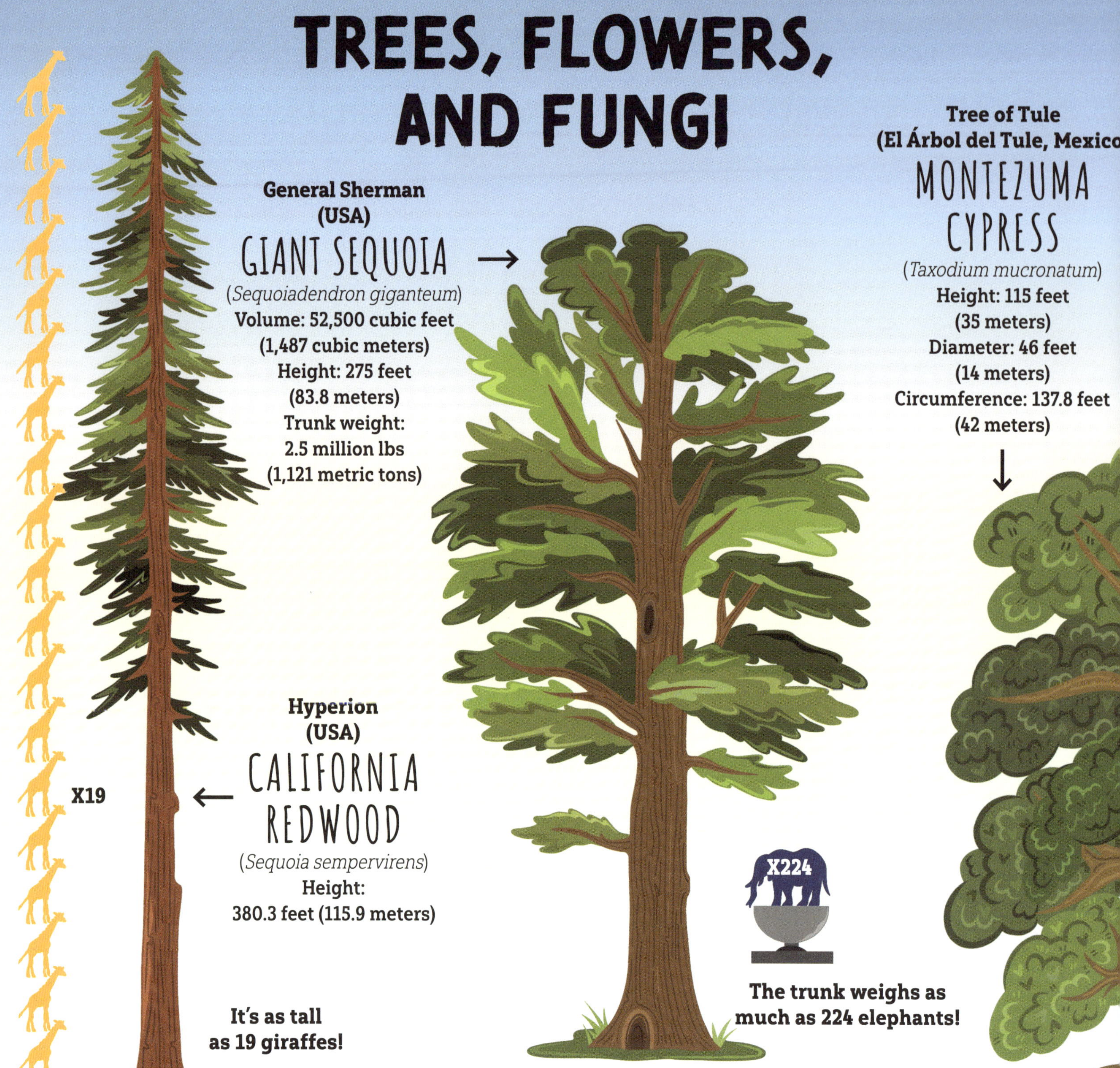

Giant flowers that stink and a baobab with a bar inside

Thinking of gifting someone a flower? You might want to avoid *Rafflesia arnoldii*. Not only is it the largest flower in the world—**it can weigh as much as a 1-year-old child** and have a **diameter 333 times the size of a daisy**—but it's also one of the smelliest, reeking of rotting flesh!

When it comes to trees, the one that takes up the most space is the **General Sherman**—a giant sequoia in California, USA. It has a volume of 52,513 cubic feet (1,487 cubic meters) and is estimated to be between 2,300 and 2,700 years old. Its trunk alone weighs about 2,471,379 lbs (1,121 metric tons)—roughly the weight of **224 African bush elephants**! But it's not the tallest tree. That title belongs to **Hyperion**, another sequoia that is taller than **19 giraffes** stacked on top of each other! To wrap your arms around the **Tree of Tule**, a gigantic Montezuma cypress in Mexico that is considered the most corpulent tree on Earth, you'd need about 24 people standing hand in hand in a human chain. But then there's the Sunland Baobab in South Africa—which, before it collapsed in 2016, had a bar and a wine cellar inside its trunk!

In India, the **banyan** tree, quite a common species there, grows in a unique way—its branches stretch horizontally, dropping aerial roots that eventually become new trunks, allowing the tree's canopy to spread wider and wider. Near the city of Kadiri, one banyan tree has grown so large that its canopy could cover **45 basketball courts**! But that's nothing compared to the **honey fungus** (*Armillaria ostoyae*), a massive organism in Malheur National Forest, Oregon (USA). This giant fungus spreads underground across 3.5 square miles—the **equivalent of 1,274 soccer fields**! Most of it lurks beneath the soil, but every now and then, it pops up as small mushrooms that resemble cloves.

LIFESPANS

Some never celebrate a birthday—others never die

Some species of insects that "live" on the surface of rivers have average lifespans of just 1–2 days. It's no surprise they're called mayflies—their scientific name, **Ephemeroptera**, comes from the Greek word for "ephemeral," meaning short-lived, and their English name implies a brief life in early spring. Meanwhile, some creatures in the cold waters of the North Atlantic, like the ocean **quahog clam** (*Arctica islandica*) and the **Greenland shark**, can survive for up to 500 years! But the undisputed (and unbeatable!) record for longevity belongs to the *Turritopsis dohrnii* jellyfish. After reaching adulthood, this jellyfish can reverse the aging process, transforming back into its juvenile polyp stage—as if a human could turn into a baby again! Because of this, it's considered potentially immortal.

1 16 20 30 60

MAYFLY
(*Ephemeroptera*)
1–2 days

MOUSE
(*Mus musculus*)
12–18 months

DOG
(*Canis lupus familiaris*)
8–16 years

CAT
(*Felis catus*)
13–20 years

HORSE
(*Equus ferus caballus*)
25–30 years

COCKATOO
(*Cacatuidae*)
40–60 years

The tree that's older than The great pyramid of giza

When the Great Pyramid of Giza was built—approximately 4,500 years ago—this tree was already standing. It is a variety of pine, ***Pinus longaeva***, found in California (USA), and it is estimated to be **4,853 years old**. It is no coincidence that it was named "Methuselah," after the legendary biblical figure said to have lived for 969 years.

70 73 100 500

AFRICAN BUSH ELEPHANT
(*Loxodonta Africana*)
60–70 years

HUMAN BEING
(*Homo sapiens*)
Average of 73 years

GALÁPAGOS GIANT TORTOISE
(*Chelonoidis nigra*)
Over 100 years

GREENLAND SHARK
(*Somniosus microcephalus*)
272–500 years

How long you live also depends on where you live

Generally speaking, it is no easy matter to determine the lifespans of animals in the wild. For animals in captivity, however, lifespans are easier to calculate and, for the most part, longer. For example, one **Galápagos giant tortoise** lived to the age of **177 years** in an Australian zoo, while a **European eel** in a Swedish aquarium lived to be **88 years** old. There have also been **dogs**, like the Australian Bluey, who've attained the age of **29 years**, and **cats**, like the American Creme Puff, who've lived to be **38 years** old. In other words, it's all relative. The same applies to human beings. The global average life expectancy is about **73 years**, but it varies significantly: people who live in Italy, one of the countries with the highest life expectancy, can hope to reach **83 years.** In contrast, in the Central African Republic, which ranks last, the average life expectancy is 30 years lower—only **54 years**. One thing is certain: thanks to medicine and healthier lifestyles, humans are living longer and longer. Until 1900, the average life expectancy at birth was just over **30 years**—about the same as in the **Paleolithic Era**! In just over 120 years, it has more than doubled, increasing by about 4 months per year. Here, too, there are records: for instance, Jeanne Calment, a French woman who passed away in 1997 at the age of 122 years.

HOW LONG DOES A

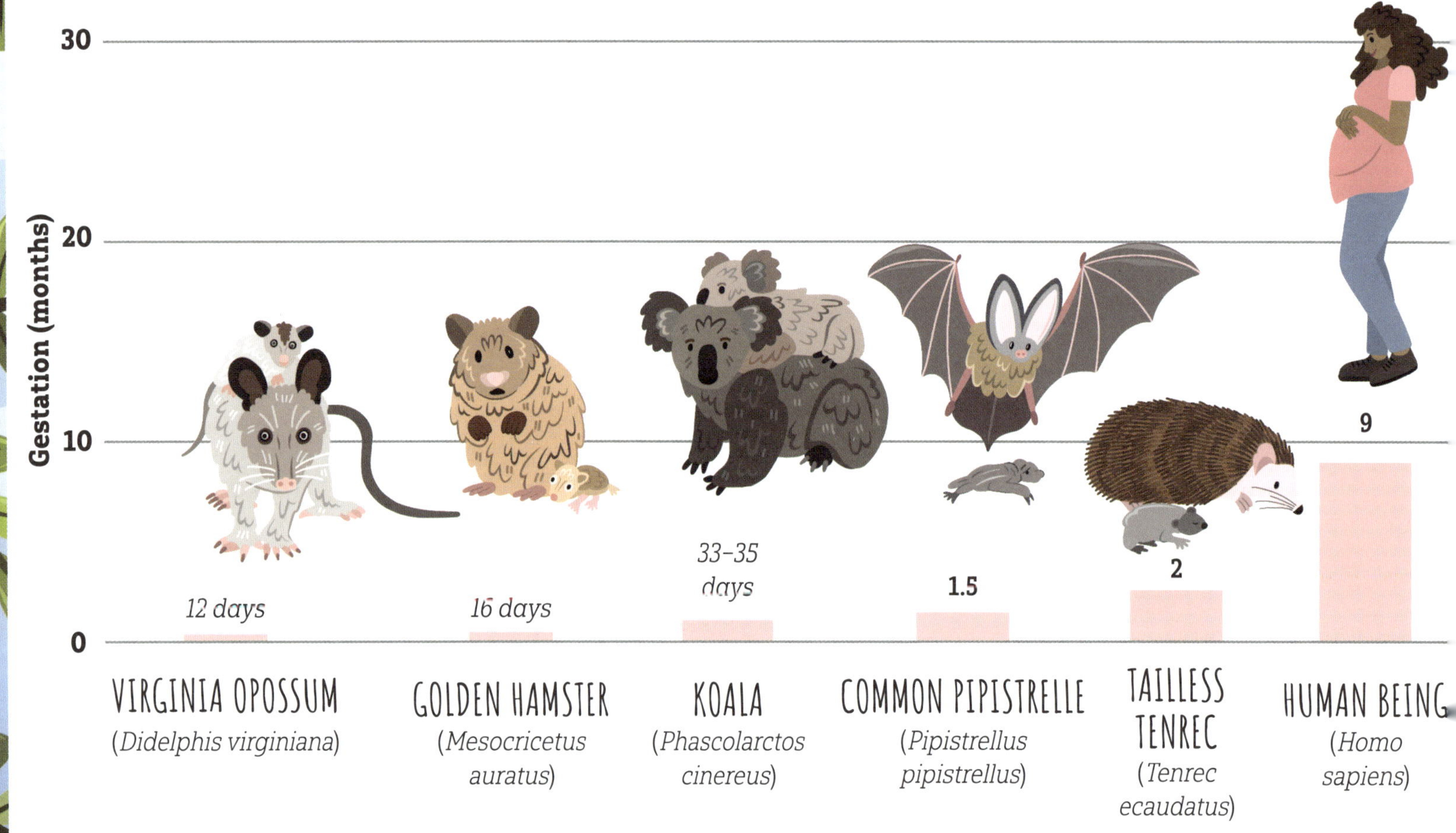

Some take just days, others over three years, and some travel Over 3,000 miles (5,000 km) to give birth

For us humans, waiting for a new sibling takes about nine months, but for a **Virginia opossum**, pregnancy lasts just 12 days. Marsupials, such as **kangaroos** and **koalas**, have very short gestation periods (that is, the period of time when an embryo remains in the mother's body)—when they are born, their babies weigh less than one gram and are no bigger than a grain of rice. They then develop inside their mother's pouch, staying there for 6 to 9 months, growing to 5,000 times their original weight—the equivalent of a human baby born at 7.7 lbs (3.5 kg) growing to the size of 35 African bush elephants (38,580 lbs / 17,500 kg) in just nine months!

Speaking of **elephants**, they hold the record for the longest mammalian pregnancy, lasting one year and eight months. When a baby elephant is born, the entire herd celebrates with trumpeting sounds. A newborn **giraffe**, on the other hand, falls to the ground from a height of 6.6 feet (2 meters) at birth. Luckily, this doesn't harm it—within 30 minutes, it can stand and start walking.

Baby **bats** are also in danger of falling—except that their mother, who gives birth upside down, catches them with her wings. Then there's the **tenrec**, a hedgehog-like mammal from Madagascar, which can give birth to 32 babies at once—a record for mammals! But even the tenrec can't compete with the **ocean sunfish** (*Mola mola*), which lays an astonishing 300 million eggs. One of the most exhausting birth processes, though, is that of the **eel**. When it's time to reproduce, eels travel 3,100 miles (5,000 km) across the Atlantic Ocean to return to the Sargasso Sea, where they were born. During this journey, they change color and stop eating altogether.

PREGNANCY LAST FOR A...

38

22

18

15

13

11

GREY SEAL
(*Halichoerus grypus*)

BACTRIAN CAMEL
(*Camelus bactrianus*)

GIRAFFE
(*Giraffa camelopardalis*)

SPERM WHALE
(*Physeter macrocephalus*)

AFRICAN BUSH ELEPHANT
(*Loxodonta Africana*)

ALPINE SALAMANDER
(*Salamandra atra aurorae*)

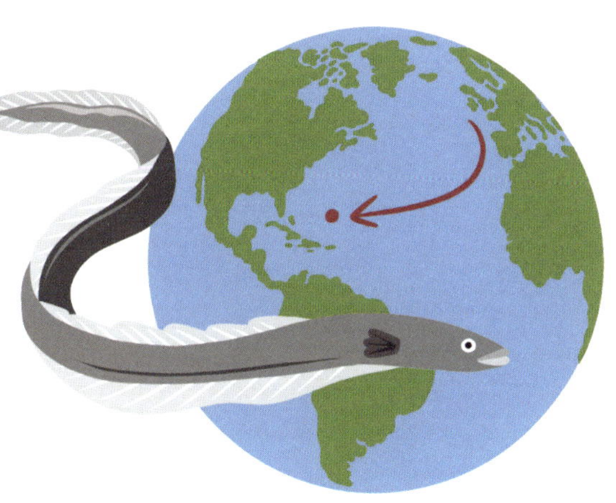

15 cm

REAL 100% SIZE

The largest egg

The **ostrich** lays the biggest eggs of any living bird. While the now-extinct moa and elephant bird laid even bigger ones, the ostrich egg measures 5.9 inches (15 cm) tall and 5.1 inches (13 cm) wide, and it weighs 3.1 lbs (1.4 kg). But in proportion to its body size, the **kiwi** lays the largest egg of all—its egg can weigh up to a quarter of its own body weight, the equivalent of a human mother giving birth to a 33-lb (15-kg) baby!

BIGGEST EATERS AND SMALLEST APPETITES

Supergluttons? Not really—it's about survival

A **blue whale** can consume up to 8,800 lbs (4 metric tons) of krill every day. With each mouthful, it swallows 457,000 kilocalories—**the equivalent of eating 1,600 Snickers bars**! But compared to its body weight, that's not so much—only about 2 percent. The **African bush elephant**, in proportion, eats a little more—around 600 lbs (270 kg) of vegetation daily, which is about 5 percent of its body weight. A real champion in terms of appetite, though, is the **giant panda**, which survives almost entirely on bamboo and spends 15–16 hours a day eating. In winter, every day it consumes leaves and stalks equal to

BLUE WHALE
(*Balaenoptera musculus*)
4.4 short tons
(4 metric tons) of krill

2.2% of its body weight

AFRICAN BUSH ELEPHANT
(*Loxodonta Africana*)
600 lbs (270 kg) of greens

5% of its body weight

GIANT PANDA
(*Ailuropoda melanoleuca*)
22–100 lbs (10–45 kg of bamboo)

15%–38%
of its body weight

15 percent of its body weight, while in summer, it prefers shoots, eating up to 100 lbs (45 kg), or 38 percent of its weight. That's nothing compared to **shrews**, which eat up to 1.5 times their own body weight every day and must eat every 2-3 hours—day and night—or risk starving to death. **Hummingbirds** are equally ravenous, feeding on insects and flower nectar. Every single day, they consume an amount of food equal to or double their body weight—which would be like a human eating 155 lbs (70 kg) of pasta, meat, vegetables, and other food every single day! But no one beats **caterpillars**—the larvae that later transform into butterflies and moths. During their short lifespan of just a couple of months, they can consume thousands of times their body weight. The Polyphemus moth caterpillar (*Antheraea polyphemus*) holds the record—eating 86,000 times its own weight before metamorphosis!

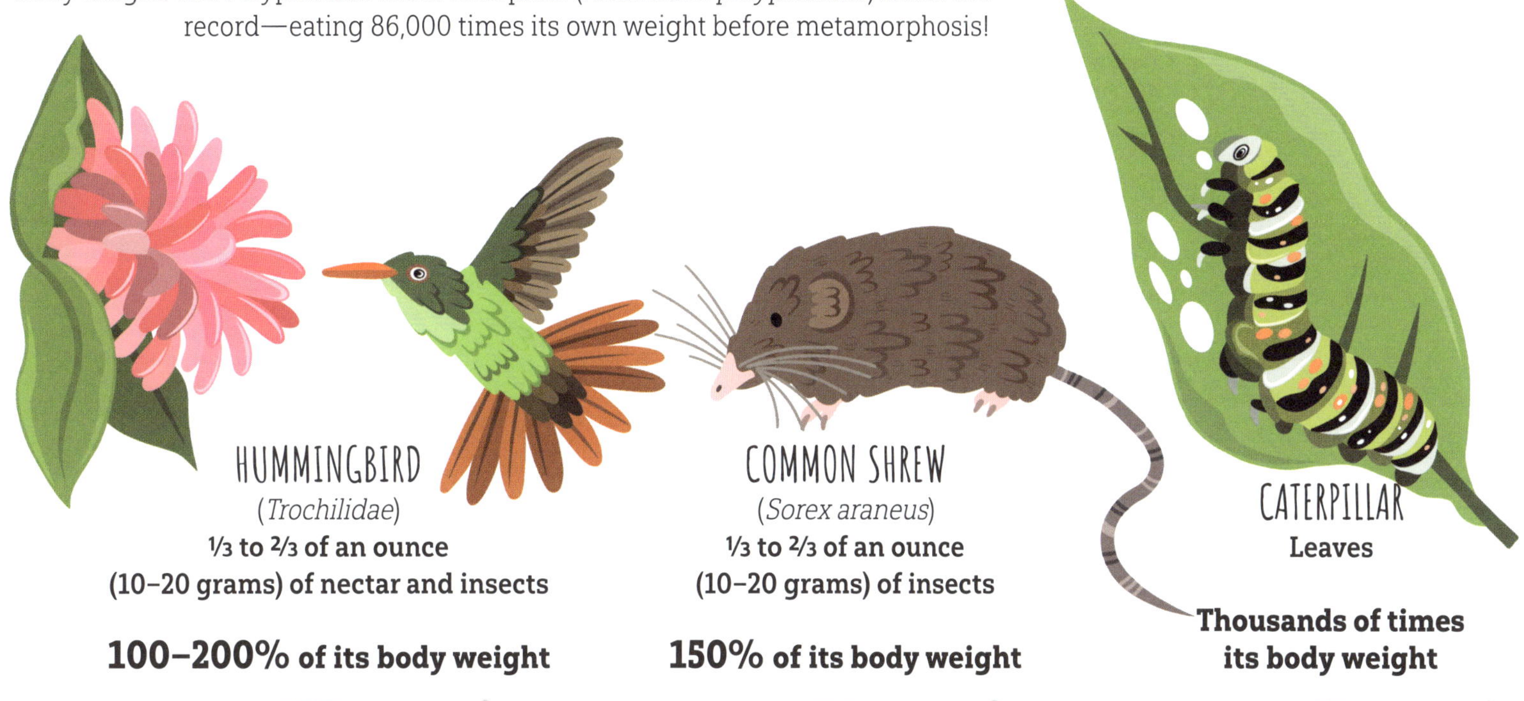

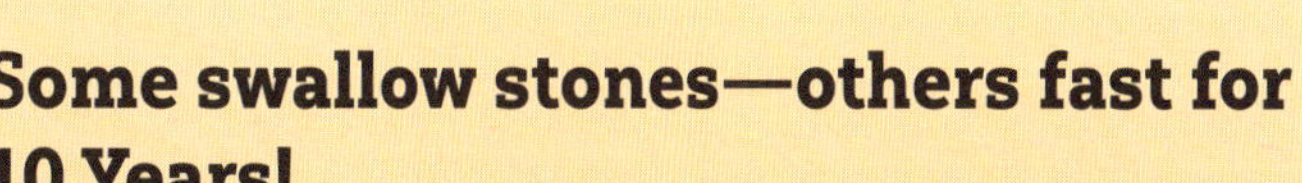

Some swallow stones—others fast for 10 Years!

Ever heard the phrase "eats anything, even rocks"? Well, the **pangolin** (*Manis*) actually does! Since it has no teeth, it swallows small stones to help grind up the thousands of ants it gulps down whole in its stomach. But how long can animals go without food? The **Bactrian camel** (*Camelus bactrianus*), thanks to its fat-filled humps, can survive for months without food and weeks without water. The **American black bear** (*Ursus americanus*) spends up to 7 months asleep during winter. Though some scientists argue it's not true hibernation, during this time it doesn't eat or drink and can lose up to 2.2 lbs (1 kg) per day, sometimes halving its total body weight over the winter. But the ultimate fasting champion is the **olm** (*Proteus anguinus*), a strange blind amphibian that lives in caves. It can go without food for a staggering 10 years!

WHO POOPS MOST—AND LEAST

The sloth? Proportionally, it poops a lot!

Lots to eat... lots to poop! It should be no surprise that the largest animal on Earth, the **blue whale** (*Balaenoptera musculus*), is also the one that produces the most poop. At a single go, it releases 50 gallons (200 liters) of liquid feces, a contribution that actually does a great deal to maintain the balance of the marine ecosystem. The **giant panda** is also a prolific pooper—it goes about 40 times a day, nearly twice an hour! The **sloth**, in contrast, poops only once a week, but when it goes, it's massive—roughly a third of its body weight. That's **like an adult human producing a 55-lb (25-kg) jumbo poop in one sitting! Snakes**, too, are slow to go. Most relieve themselves a couple of days after feeding, but some can hold it in for months, sometimes longer than a year. The record is held by a Gaboon viper (*Bitis gabonica*), which went 1 year and 55 days without pooping!

Besides producing it, some animals actually eat poop. Gross as that may sound, coprophagy (the act of eating feces) is quite common in nature. Elephants, pandas, koalas, gorillas, hamsters, rabbits, piglets, and even dogs do it. In fact, dogs love cat poop because it's rich in protein. But the most famous poop eaters are dung beetles, which feed on nothing but feces. What about humans? We're not entirely innocent either. One of the world's most expensive and prized coffees, kopi luwak, is made using coffee beans that have passed through the digestive system of the Asian palm civet (*Paradoxurus hermaphroditus*). Yep... it's coffee made from poop.

GIANT PANDA
(*Ailuropoda melanoleuca*)
40 times a day

AFRICAN BUSH ELEPHANT
(*Loxodonta Africana*)
12–15 times a day

COW
(*Bos taurus*)
15 times a day

DUCK
(*Anas platyrhynchos domesticus*)
Every 15–30 minutes

Believe it or not, the white sand on some of those breathtaking tropical beaches you see in travel ads is actually made of parrotfish poop! These colorful fish, like *Chlorurus gibbus*, feed on algae growing on coral reefs. As they graze, they also nibble off bits of coral, digest them, and then excrete tiny grains of coral sand, which eventually form beaches. According to scientists, a single parrotfish can produce over 2,000 lbs (one metric ton) of sand per year!

Beaches aside, animal poop is invaluable for scientists, as well. By analyzing feces, researchers can learn what animals eat, assess their health, estimate population sizes, and track their movements across different habitats. And it's not just about living animals. Even creatures that disappeared millions of years ago can be studied through **coprolites**—fossilized poop that long ago turned to stone!

WHO SLEEPS THE MOST AND WHO SLEEPS THE LEAST

Some use their bottoms as pillows—others sleep while flying

Giraffes sleep for an average of 4.5 hours per day, taking short naps of about 30 minutes at a time. When they do, they usually remain standing, with half-closed eyes and their long necks bent downward, almost as if they were using their own backsides as pillows! **Crocodiles**, on the other hand, sleep with one eye open to keep an eye out for prey and potential dangers. This is called unihemispheric sleep, meaning that only one hemisphere of the brain rests at a time. The same happens with **dolphins**, whose half-awake brains allow them to remain alert while they sleep. Certain birds, like the **Alpine swift** (*Tachymarptis melba*), can even fly for up to 200 days straight! When they don't need to flap their wings much and can glide through the air, they take quick power naps mid-flight. Fish, too, need rest. While most stay somewhat alert to protect themselves from predators, some actually seem to sleep. The **zebrafish** (*Danio rerio*), for example, stops swimming and floats motionless when resting. Meanwhile, **heavybeak parrotfish** (*Chlorurus gibbus*) protect themselves at night by wrapping themselves in a mucus cocoon that they secrete—essentially, a self-made sleeping bag! The **walrus** is one of the sleepiest creatures, alongside the **koala** and the **little brown bat**. It sleeps most of the day, either floating in the water, resting against a surface, or—amazingly—hooking itself onto an ice sheet with its long tusks! Meanwhile, sperm whales (*Physeter macrocephalus*) take naps by sleeping vertically in the water. Each species has its favorite sleeping position, just like humans. On average, an adult **human** sleeps 8 hours per day, while children (up to age 12) need 9 to 12 hours, and older adults average just 5.5 hours.

DOG
(*Canis lupus familiaris*)

CAT
(*Felis catus*)

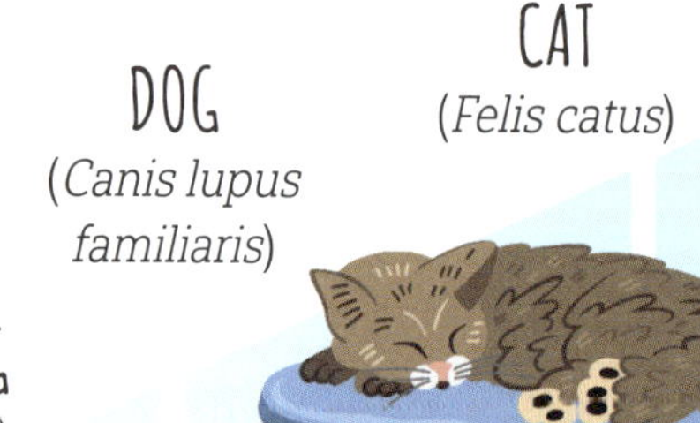

12 hours

HUMAN BEING
(*Homo sapiens*)

10.5 hours

8 hours

SHORT-BEAKED COMMON DOLPHIN
(*Delphinus delphis*)

HORSE
(*Equus ferus caballus*)

4.5 hours

3 hours

GIRAFFE
(*Giraffa camelopardalis*)

2 hours

Never entirely

AFRICAN BUSH ELEPHANT
(*Loxodonta Africana*)

LITTLE BROWN BAT
(*Myotis lucifugus*)

22 hours

GIANT ARMADILLO
(*Priodontes maximus*)

DUCK-BILLED PLATYPUS
(*Ornithorhynchus anatinus*)

SNAIL

20 hours

18 hours

KOALA
(*Phascolarctos cinereus*)

15 hours

14 hours

WALRUS
(*Odobenus rosmarus*)

SQUIRREL
(*Sciurus*)

Do you sleep like a dormouse, a snail, or a lungfish?

Many animals go into hibernation, which is called "estivation" if it happens in summer and "brumation" if it occurs in autumn. This is a state of torpor, different from sleep, where all vital functions slow down to help the animal conserve as much energy as possible.

The **Alpine marmot** (*Marmota marmota*) hibernates for 8 months, during which it breathes only 2–3 times per minute, and its heart slows to 3–4 beats per minute—a huge drop from its normal 120 beats per minute. The **European edible dormouse** (*Glis glis*) also hibernates for about 8 months, but in certain conditions, it can sleep for up to 11 months. No wonder people say "to sleep like a mouse"! But maybe the saying should be "to sleep like a snail"! Some **snails** living in dry environments bury themselves underground and can stay in hibernation for years. And the real champions of survival? The **African lungfish** (*Dipnoi*). These fish can survive up to 4 years without water, burying themselves in mud and breathing air through a fully developed lung—which is why they're called lungfish.

HUMAN STRUCTURES

HUMANS HAVE CREATED INCREDIBLY FAST VEHICLES, GIGANTIC BUILDINGS, SKYSCRAPERS ALMOST AS TALL AS MOUNTAINS, AND CITIES SO VAST THAT THEY HOLD AS MANY PEOPLE AS AN ENTIRE COUNTRY. FOR EXAMPLE, IF YOU COMBINED THE POPULATIONS OF JUST TWO CITIES—TOKYO AND NEW YORK—YOU COULD FILL ALL OF ITALY!

ROADS

The longest, the narrowest, the widest, and the oldest roads

It's estimated that the total length of all roads on Earth would be enough to travel **to the Moon and back 83 times**. Perhaps that calculation includes the 7.5-mile (12-kilometer) road that starts at Lake Qarun and was built in ancient Egypt to transport basalt blocks from a nearby quarry. Dating back 4,500 years, it is considered the oldest paved road ever discovered. The country with the most roads? The **United States**. If you added up all its roads, you could circle the Earth **171 times at the equator**. **India** and **China**, ranking second and third, also have vast networks. Meanwhile, despite being the largest country in the world, **Russia** ranks only fifth, with 930,000 miles (1.5 million km) of roads. By comparison, France—which is 31 times smaller than Russia but has the longest road network in Europe—has far more roads (while Italy ranks 17th). The longest single road in the world is the **Pan-American Highway**, which begins in Alaska and, after crossing two continents (North and South America), reaches Ushuaia, Argentina—the second-southernmost city in the world after Puerto Williams. The only break in the route is a 62-mile (100-kilometer) gap in the Darién Gap, a dense forest and swamp region between Panama and Colombia. Driving the entire 19,000-mile (30,000-km) route at an average speed of 75 mph (120 km/h)—without ever stopping to sleep or even take a bathroom break—**would take about 10.5 days**. By contrast, it takes only two minutes to cross **Avenida 9 de Julio** in Buenos Aires, Argentina, at a normal walking pace. But that's no small feat—it's considered the widest road in the world, stretching 360 feet (110 meters) across, roughly the **length of a soccer field**! And the narrowest? That would be **Spreuerhofstraße**, a tiny alley in Reutlingen, Germany, that measures just 12 inches (31 cm) wide—barely wider than this page!

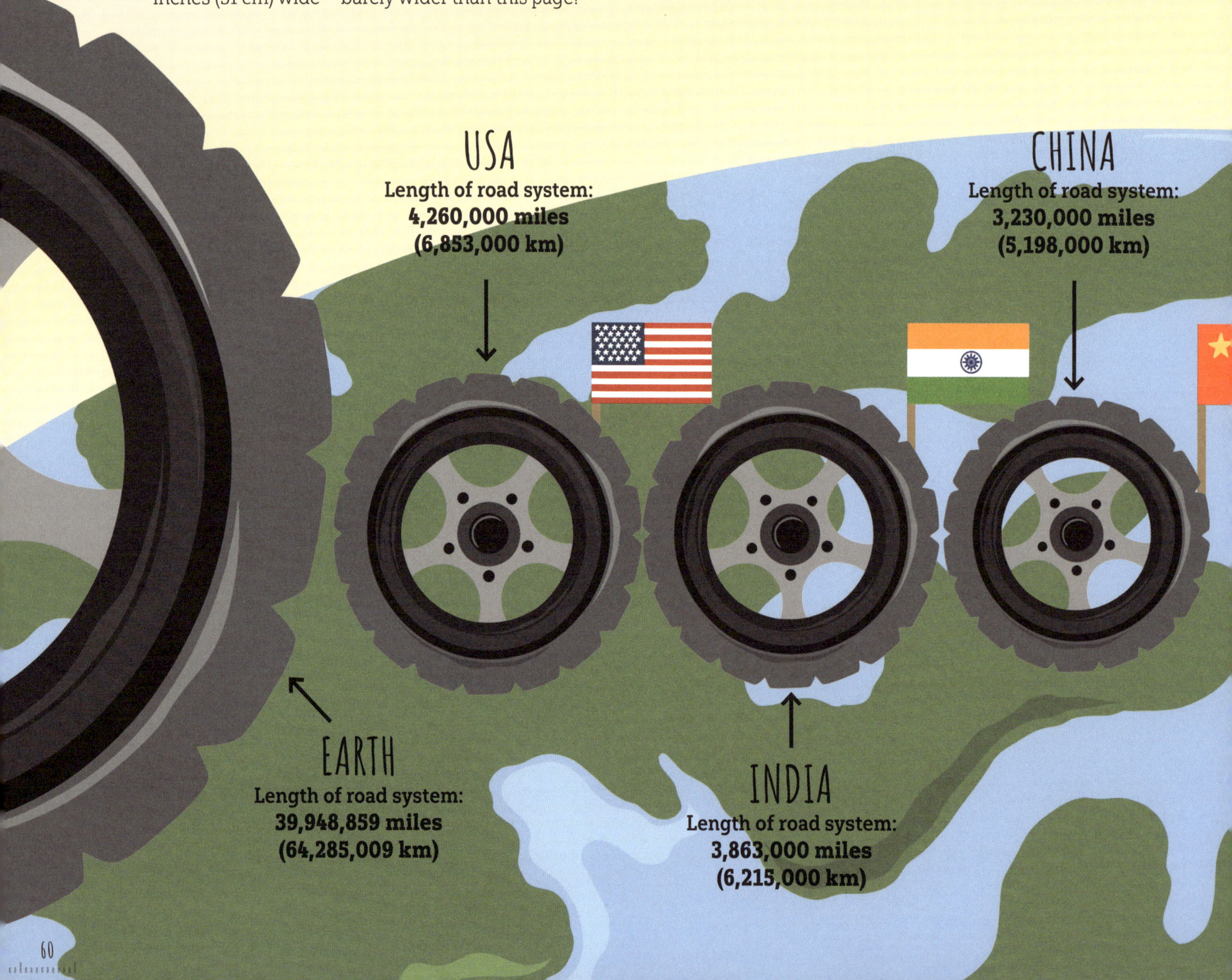

THE WORLD'S LONGEST ROAD TUNNEL

If tunnels make you a little anxious and you can't wait to get out every time you enter one, then you might want to avoid the route from Lærdal to Aurland in Norway. These two towns are connected by the longest road tunnel in the world. Opened in 2000, it stretches 15.25 miles (24.51 km) in length. If there's no traffic and you stick to the speed limit of 50 mph (80 km/h), it takes about **20 minutes** to drive through. On foot? That would take around six hours!

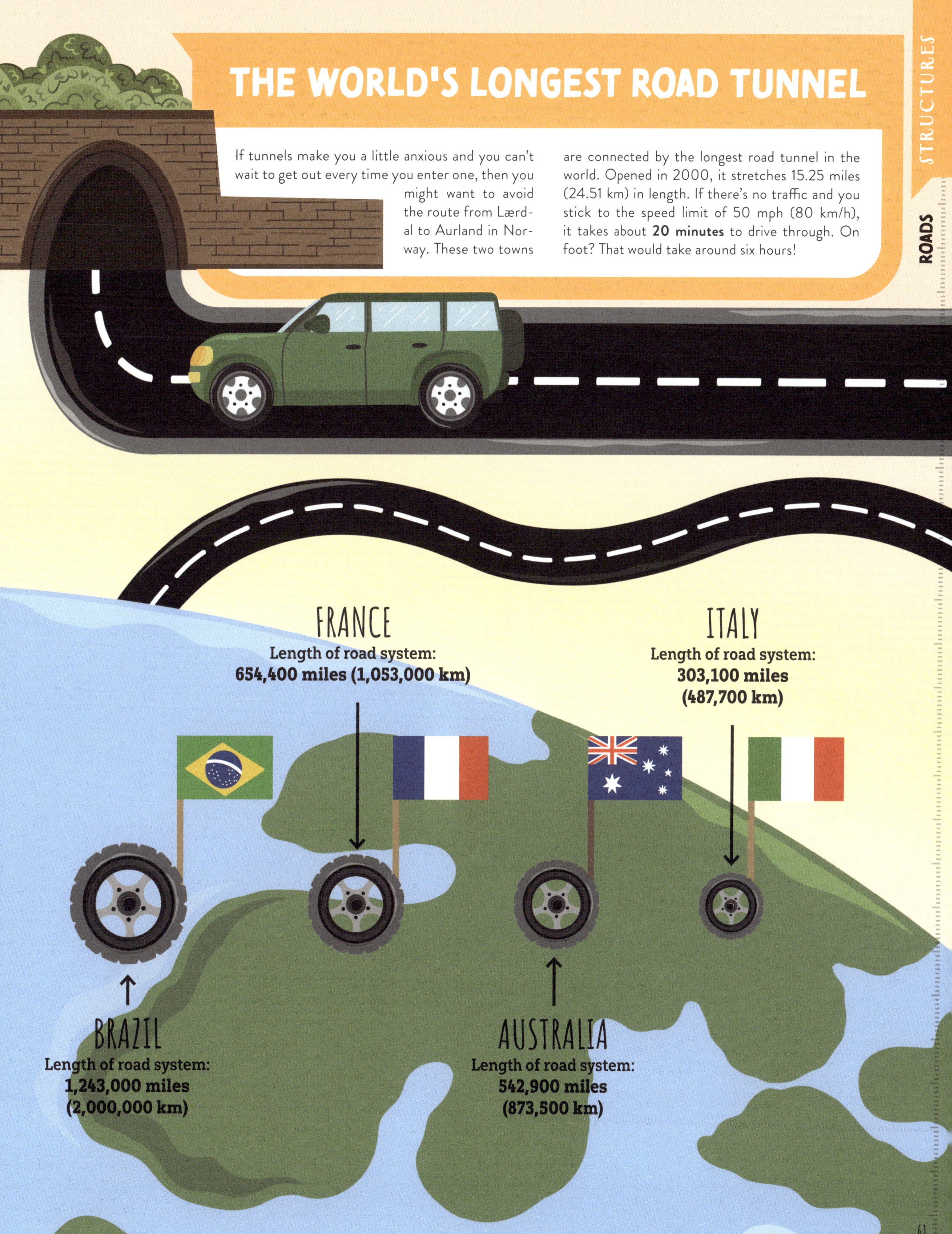

RAILS

The longest train

682 CARS

Even though others have tried to beat its record, the longest passenger train still in operation is **The Ghan** in Australia. This famous train takes tourists on a 1,860-mile (3,000-km) journey from north to south, a trip lasting over two days, including stops for sightseeing. During peak travel seasons, it consists of 44 carriages and 2 locomotives, reaching a total length of 3,600 feet (1,100 meters)—about as **long as 80 buses lined up in a row**! In total, it weighs 4,753,000 lbs (2,156 metric tons)—the **equivalent of 431 elephants**! But even The Ghan is nothing compared to freight trains. In Australia, iron ore mines transport materials using trains almost 1.85 miles (3 km) long, made up of 268 wagons. In 2001, however, a record-breaking train was used, consisting of a staggering 682 carriages, stretching 4.57 miles (7,353 meters)—longer than the height of Aconcagua, the tallest mountain in South America at 22,838 feet (6,961 meters)! Walking from the front to the back of this train would take about an hour and a half!

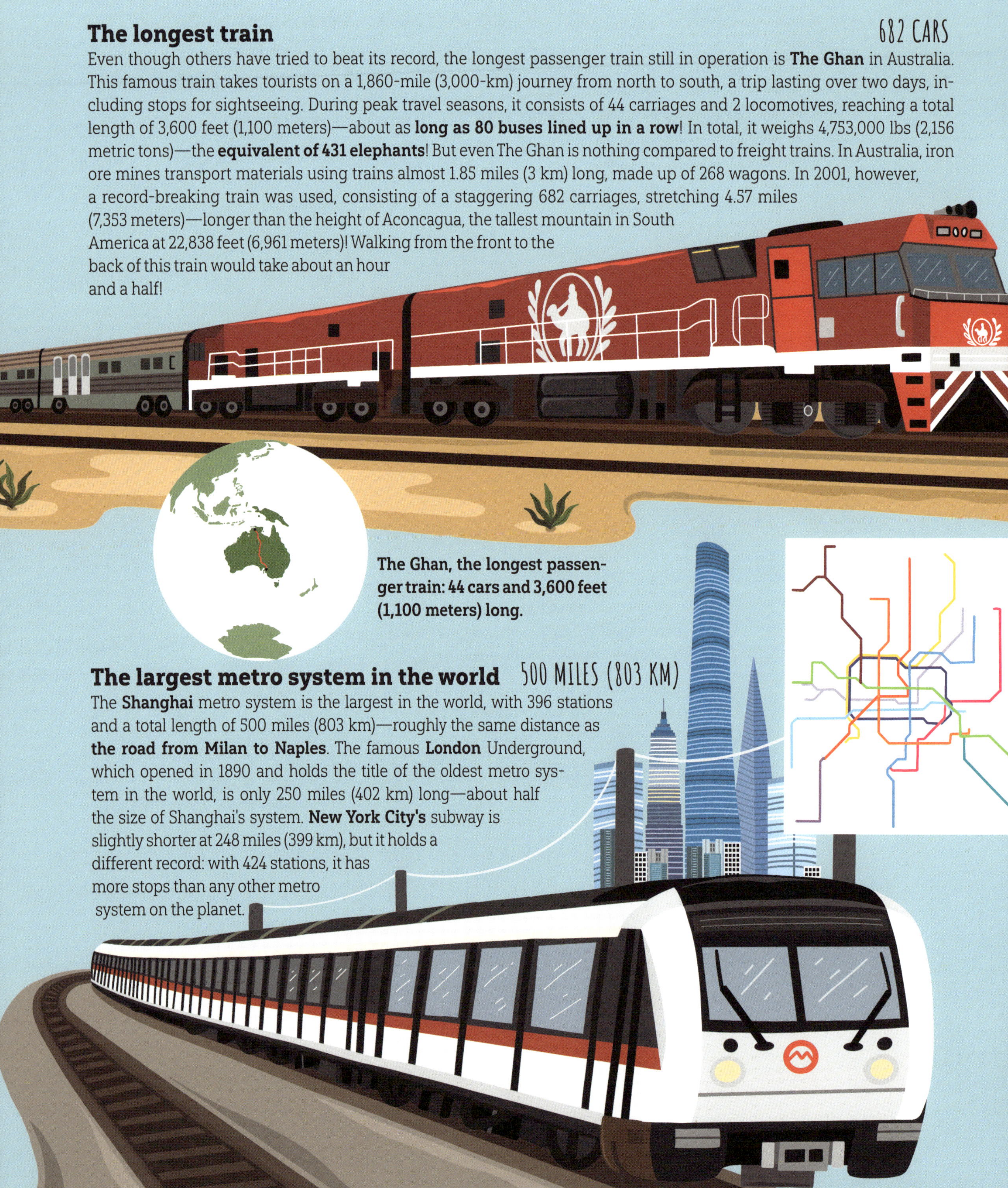

The Ghan, the longest passenger train: 44 cars and 3,600 feet (1,100 meters) long.

The largest metro system in the world

500 MILES (803 KM)

The **Shanghai** metro system is the largest in the world, with 396 stations and a total length of 500 miles (803 km)—roughly the same distance as **the road from Milan to Naples**. The famous **London** Underground, which opened in 1890 and holds the title of the oldest metro system in the world, is only 250 miles (402 km) long—about half the size of Shanghai's system. **New York City's** subway is slightly shorter at 248 miles (399 km), but it holds a different record: with 424 stations, it has more stops than any other metro system on the planet.

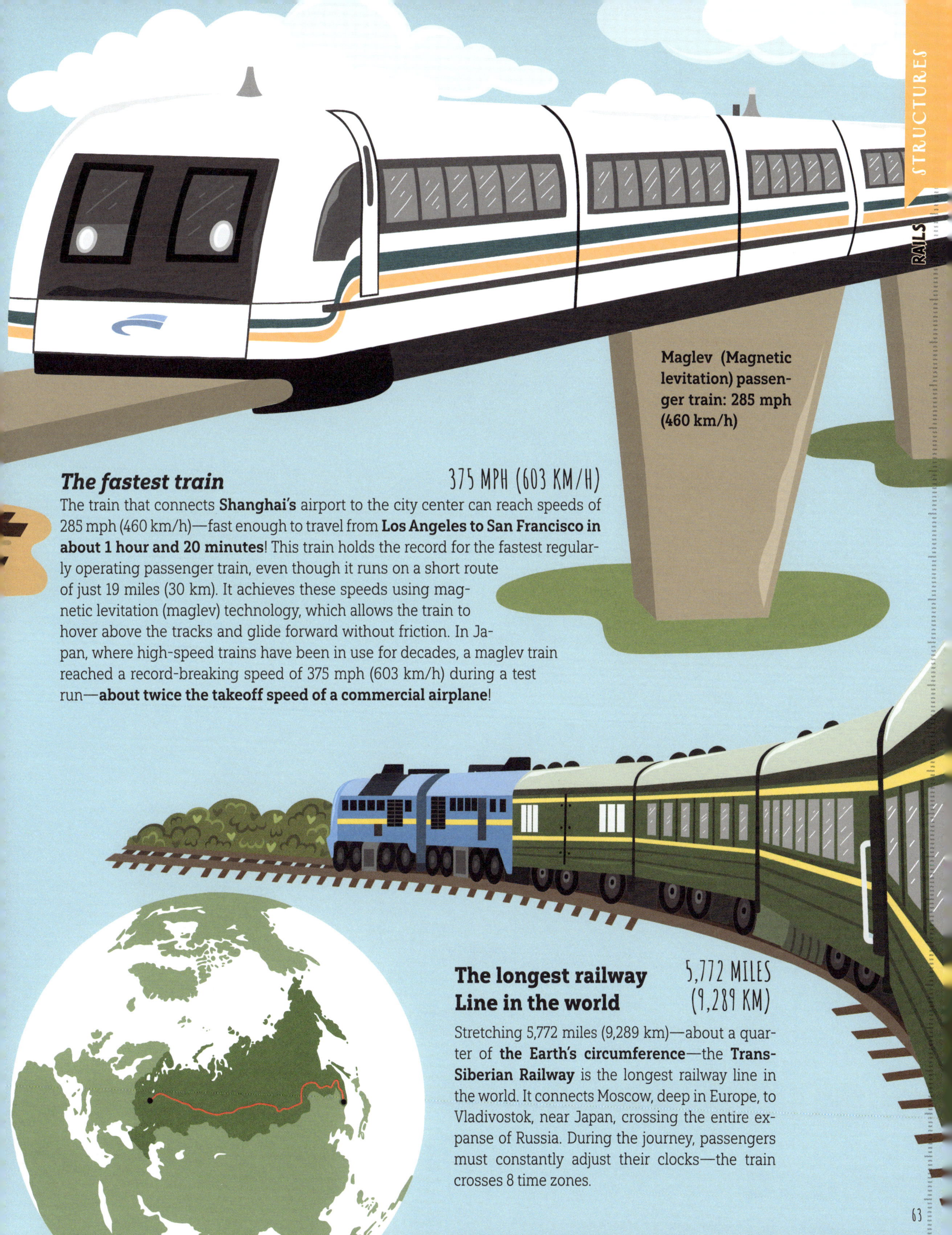

The fastest train

375 MPH (603 KM/H)

The train that connects **Shanghai's** airport to the city center can reach speeds of 285 mph (460 km/h)—fast enough to travel from **Los Angeles to San Francisco in about 1 hour and 20 minutes**! This train holds the record for the fastest regularly operating passenger train, even though it runs on a short route of just 19 miles (30 km). It achieves these speeds using magnetic levitation (maglev) technology, which allows the train to hover above the tracks and glide forward without friction. In Japan, where high-speed trains have been in use for decades, a maglev train reached a record-breaking speed of 375 mph (603 km/h) during a test run—**about twice the takeoff speed of a commercial airplane**!

The longest railway Line in the world

5,772 MILES (9,289 KM)

Stretching 5,772 miles (9,289 km)—about a quarter of **the Earth's circumference**—the **Trans-Siberian Railway** is the longest railway line in the world. It connects Moscow, deep in Europe, to Vladivostok, near Japan, crossing the entire expanse of Russia. During the journey, passengers must constantly adjust their clocks—the train crosses 8 time zones.

MEANS OF TRANSPORTATION

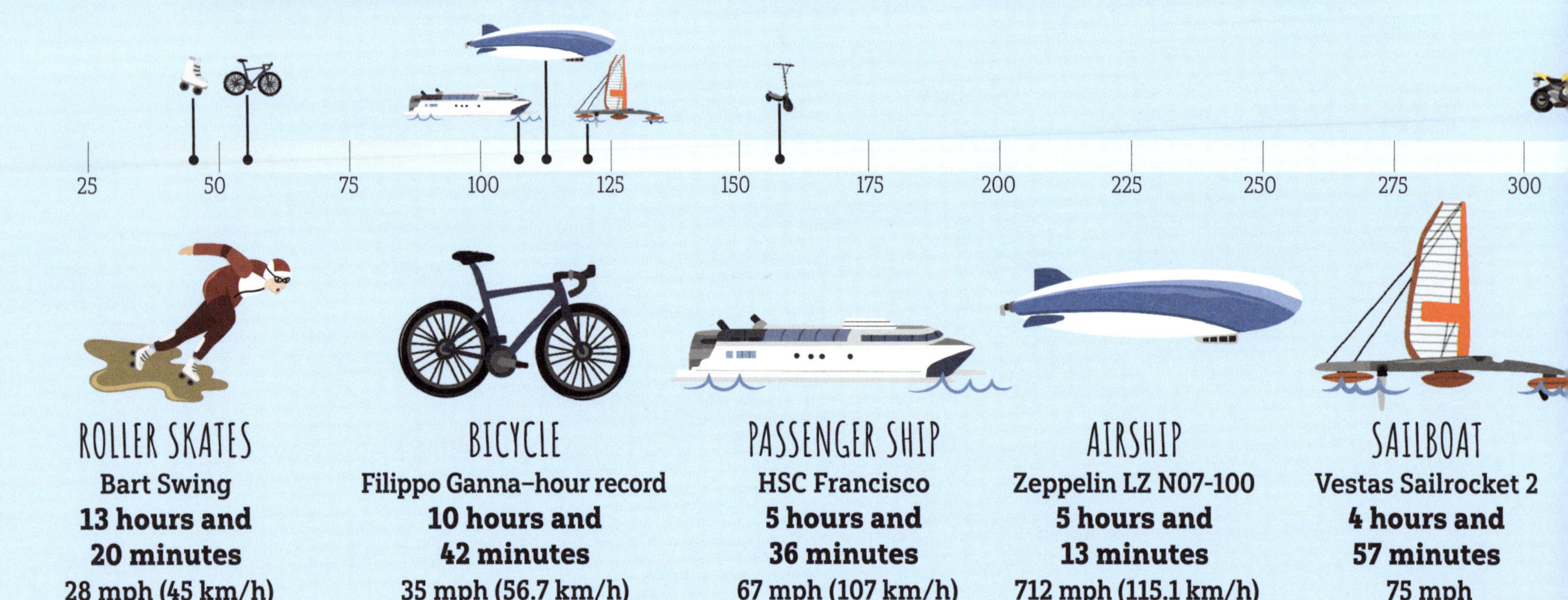

ROLLER SKATES
Bart Swing
13 hours and 20 minutes
28 mph (45 km/h)

BICYCLE
Filippo Ganna–hour record
10 hours and 42 minutes
35 mph (56.7 km/h)

PASSENGER SHIP
HSC Francisco
5 hours and 36 minutes
67 mph (107 km/h)

AIRSHIP
Zeppelin LZ N07-100
5 hours and 13 minutes
712 mph (115.1 km/h)

SAILBOAT
Vestas Sailrocket 2
4 hours and 57 minutes
75 mph (121.1 km/h)

Higher and higher—all the way to space

In 2014, an Australian named Robert Moore flew a kite to an altitude of 16,007 feet (4,879 meters)—**higher than Mont Blanc** and even higher than the hang-gliding record set by Austrian Anton Raumauf in 2016. The kite itself was 129 square feet (12 square meters) in size—**about as large as three ping-pong tables**—with a wingspan of 20 feet (6 meters), roughly the same as two snowy albatrosses. It was tethered to a large electric winch that controlled its ascent. In 2005, during a rescue mission, a helicopter landed on Mount Everest at more than 26,250 feet (8,000 meters)—a record for helicopter landings. But there is someone who's flown even higher. In 2002, Fred North, a pilot who has worked on many action films, reached an astonishing altitude of 42,500 feet (12,954 meters)—about three miles (5,000 meters) higher than the usual limit for helicopters. And that's still nothing compared to hot air balloons, gliders, and various types of aircraft, including *SpaceShipOne*, an experimental vehicle that soared to 70 miles (112 km)—beyond the official boundary of space, which scientists define as 62 miles (100 km) above Earth. It's no coincidence that *SpaceShipOne* was powered by a rocket—escaping Earth's gravity is no easy feat. To do so, a rocket must reach a velocity of about 25,000 mph (40,000 km/h), follow the correct trajectory, and, ideally, avoid burning up everything and everyone on board. One of the most famous rockets ever built, the *Saturn V*, carried the first astronauts to the Moon in 1969. It stood 364 feet (111 meters) tall, **about the same as a 36-story building**, and when fully fueled, it weighed six million pounds (2.8 million kg)—the **equivalent of 560 elephants**. Just the fuel alone was enough to fill one-and-a-half Olympic swimming pools!

How long would it take me to go from Washington DC to Boston by...?

This is how long it would take you to travel 375 miles (600 km, or from Washington DC to Boston) if you could travel without traffic, never have to slow down, and maintain the top speed available to each means of transportation.

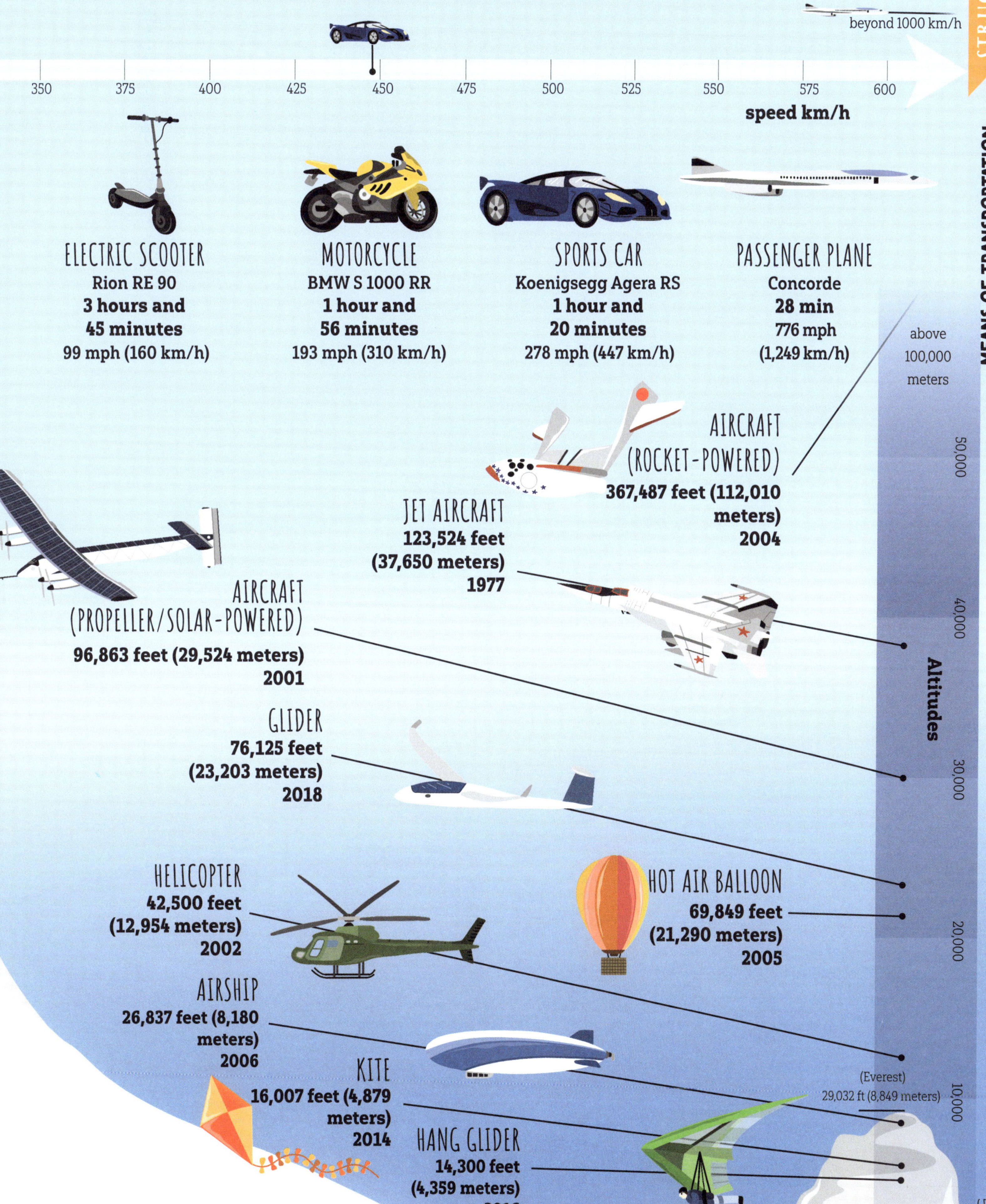

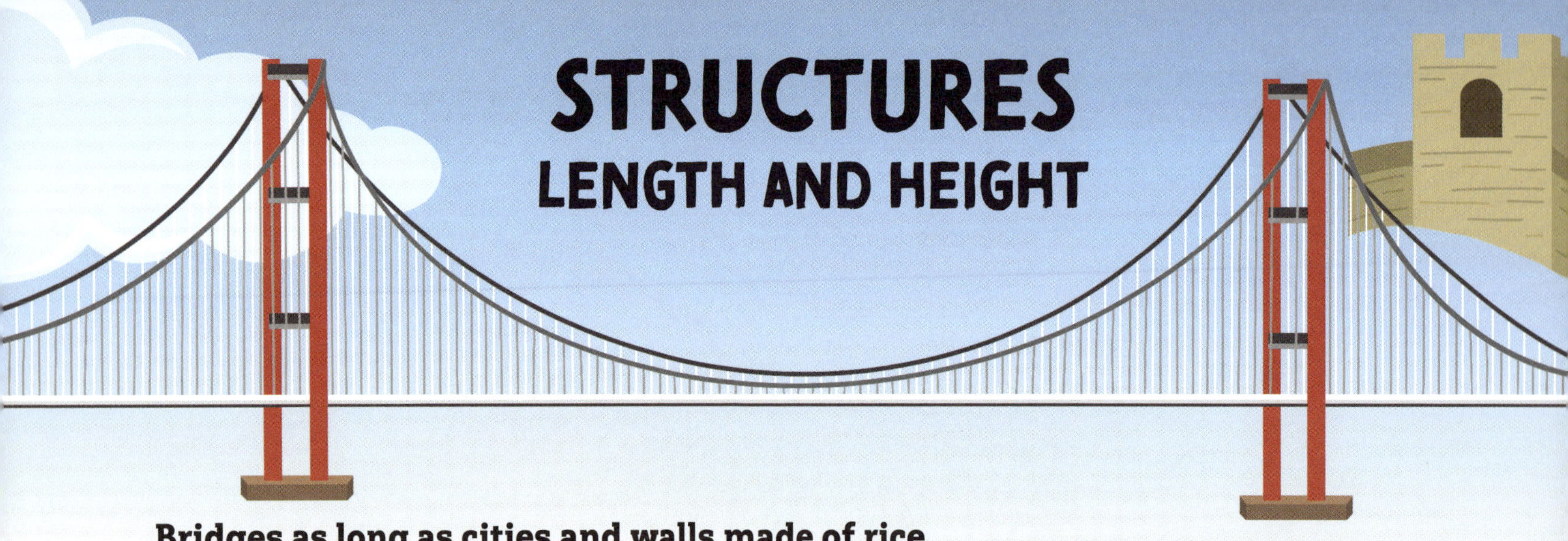

STRUCTURES

LENGTH AND HEIGHT

Bridges as long as cities and walls made of rice

What is the longest bridge in the world? That all depends on how you're measuring bridges. If we consider the longest single span—the distance between two supporting towers—then the record belongs to the **Dardanelles Bridge** (or 1915 Çanakkale Köprüsü) in Turkey, which was inaugurated in March 2022. With a span of 6,637 feet (2,023 meters), it surpassed Japan's **Akashi-Kaikyō Bridge**, the previous record holder. To visualize it, imagine placing a single wooden plank across a river, but one **as long as 18 soccer fields**! The longest bridge overall, however, is the **Danyang-Kunshan Grand Bridge** in China, a railway viaduct that runs parallel to the Yangtze River for much of its length. It stretches an incredible 102.5 miles (165 km)—roughly the same distance as a drive from **Philadelphia to Baltimore, Maryland**. Still, that's nothing compared to the **Great Wall of China**, which is 128 times longer. According to the latest estimates, this massive defensive structure built in ancient China is 13,171 miles (21,196 km) long—**more than half Earth's circumference**! It is considered one of the greatest human-made structures ever built, but no, you cannot see it from the Moon with the naked eye, no matter what urban legends claim. What is true, however, is that the wall is partly made of rice! To build it, workers used a glutinous variety of rice, rich in starch. When cooked and mixed with powdered limestone, it created a kind of ancient cement.

An elevator to the sky

Kingda Ka, a legendary roller coaster in New Jersey, USA, closed in 2024. In just 3.5 seconds, it reached 128 mph (206 km/h)—a Formula 1 race car takes roughly twice as long to reach that speed! It also held the record as the tallest roller coaster in the world, standing at 456 feet (139 meters)—as tall as Egypt's **Great Pyramid of Giza**, which remained the tallest human-made structure for 3,800 years. When it comes to amusement park rides, though, the record belongs to the **Ain Dubai** Ferris wheel in Dubai, which stands 820 feet (250 meters) tall—the **height of an 83-story building**. That's nothing compared to the **Burj Khalifa**, also in Dubai, which is the tallest structure in the world. At 2,719 feet (829 meters)—nearly three times the height of the **Eiffel Tower** (1,083 feet/330 meters)—it dominates the skyline like no other building. It contains 57 elevators, including the one with the longest travel distance in the world—a single 1,653-foot (504-meter) ride!

ROLLER COASTER
Kingda Ka
456 feet
(139 meters)
(USA)
←

TOWER
Leaning Tower of Pisa
2,183 ft (56 meters)
(Italy)
→

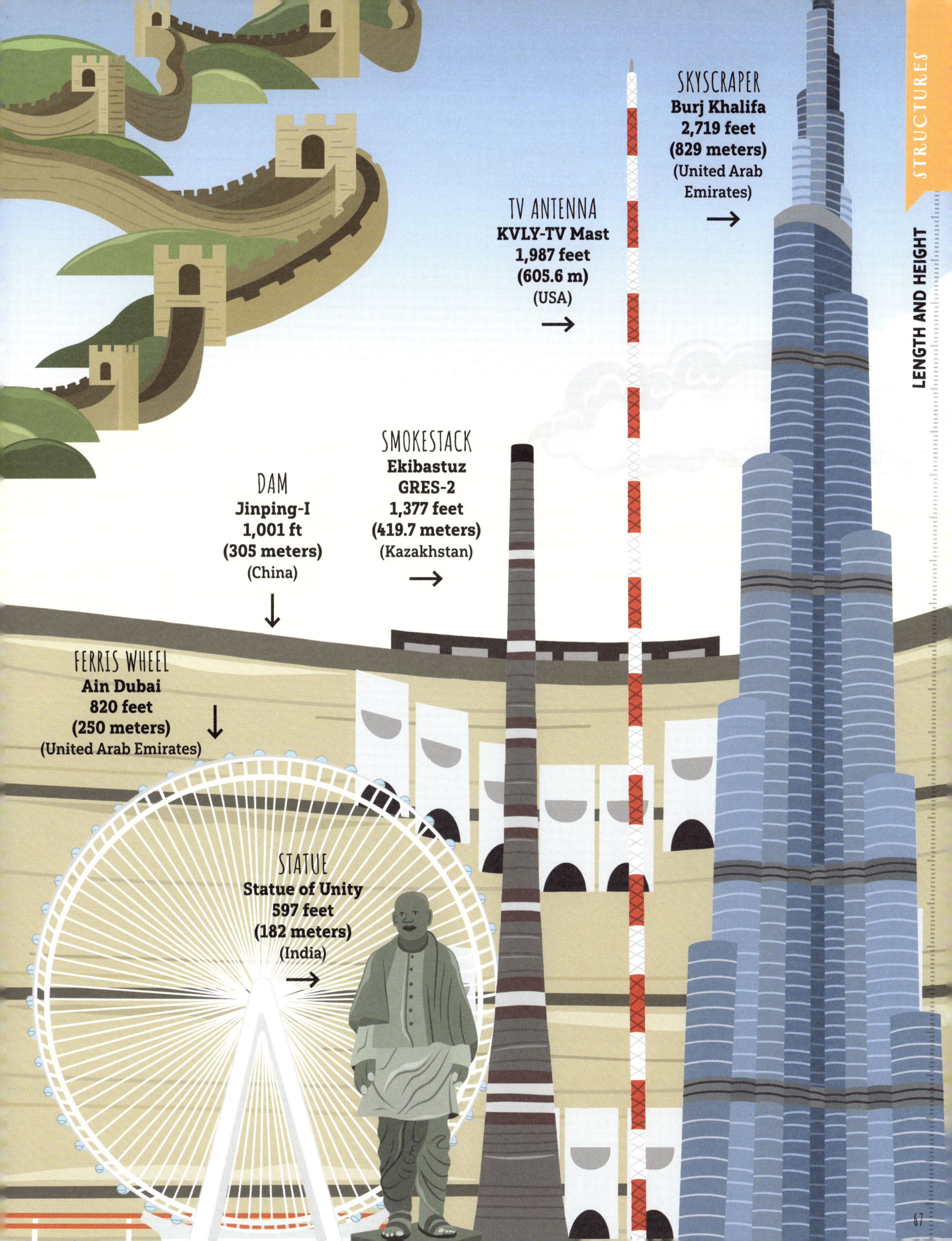
SKYSCRAPER
Burj Khalifa
2,719 feet
(829 meters)
(United Arab Emirates)
TV ANTENNA
KVLY-TV Mast
1,987 feet
(605.6 m)
(USA)
SMOKESTACK
Ekibastuz GRES-2
1,377 feet
(419.7 meters)
(Kazakhstan)
DAM
Jinping-I
1,001 ft
(305 meters)
(China)
FERRIS WHEEL
Ain Dubai
820 feet
(250 meters)
(United Arab Emirates)
STATUE
Statue of Unity
597 feet
(182 meters)
(India)

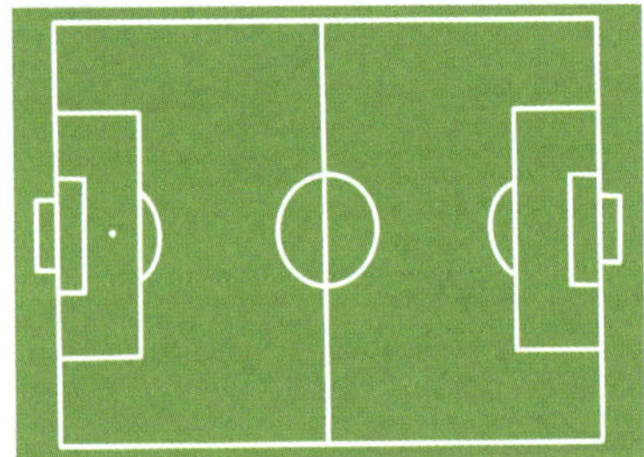

STRUCTURES
FOOTPRINT

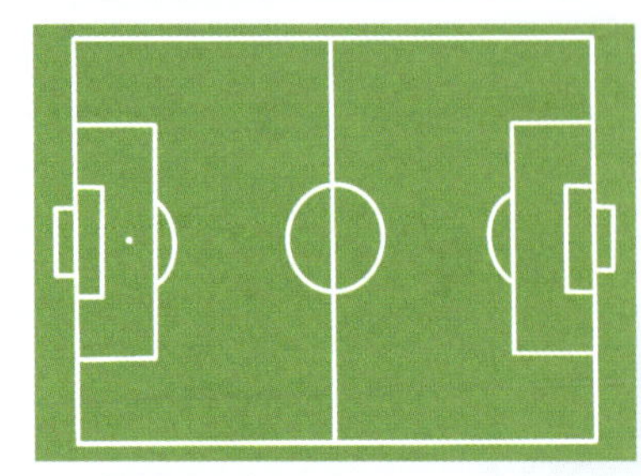

LARGEST RELIGIOUS EDIFICE

Angkor Wat
(Angkor, Cambodia)

17,502,000 sq. ft
(1,626,000 sq. m.)

Like **228** soccer fields

LARGEST FACTORY

Giga Texas
(Austin, United States)

10,000,000 sq. ft.
(930,000 sq. m.)

Like **130** soccer fields

LARGEST OFFICE BUILDING

Pentagon
(Arlington County, Virginia, USA)

6,500,000 sq. ft.
(620,000 sq. m.)

Like **87** soccer fields

A building as heavy as 21,500 blue whales

To match the weight of the **Palace of Parliament** in Bucharest, Romania, you would need to place about **21,500 blue whales** on a giant scale. Completed in 1997 after 13 years of construction, it is in fact considered the heaviest building in the world and also one of the largest, covering an area roughly equivalent to **51 soccer fields**. But when it comes to sheer size, **the temple of Angkor Wat** in Cambodia holds the record. Built in 1150 to honor the Hindu god Vishnu, it occupies an area roughly **half the size of Central Park** in New York—making it the largest religious complex in the world. That's far bigger than **Tesla's** Gigafactory in Austin, Texas, which is the world's largest building by occupied surface area. By comparison, the **International Space Station** (ISS) is tiny, with a surface area only just larger than a soccer field. Building it, however, was no easy feat—it orbits Earth at about 17,000 mph (27,000 km/h)! Because of that speed, astronauts on board experience **16 sunrises and sunsets per day, one every 45 minutes**.

LARGEST PALACE

Palace of Parliament
(Bucharest, Romania)

3,930,000 sq. ft.
(365,000 sq. m.)

Like **51** soccer fields

LARGEST MUSEUM

Louvre
(Paris, France)

2,260,000 sq. ft.
(210,000 sq. m.)

Like **29** soccer fields

LARGEST CHURCH

St. Peter's Basilica
(Vatican City)

237,527 sq. ft.
(22,067 sq. m.)

Like **3** soccer fields

International Space Station

85,573 sq. ft.
(7,950 sq. m.)

Like **1.1** soccer fields

THE OLDEST STRUCTURE EVER BUILT

In Greece, inside **Theopetra Cave**, where humans lived 130,000 years ago, archaeologists have found what is considered the oldest known human-made structure—a 23,000-year-old wall, likely built to block cold winds. That makes it 18,000 years older than the Great Pyramid of Giza.

When it comes to elaborate stone structures, the oldest known stone temple is **Göbekli Tepe** in Turkey, built between 10,000 and 12,000 years ago—before agriculture and animal domestication became widespread. The site contains massive stone pillars, each weighing up to 44,000 lbs (20 metric tons), some intricately decorated with carvings of animals (foxes, leopards, snakes...). Archaeologists continue to study them to understand their meaning.

CITIES

Italy? You could fill it with just two megacities

Today, 57% of the world's population lives in cities, and that number is expected to keep growing. By 2050, nearly two-thirds of the global population will live in urban areas. But how do we count a city's population? It depends on where you draw the borders. Some count only legal city limits, while others include surrounding metropolitan areas. For example, Milan officially has 1.37 million inhabitants, but if you include its greater metropolitan area, that number jumps to 5.5 million—four times as many! Even considering these differences, would you have guessed that **Tokyo and New York City together have enough people to fill all of Italy**?

These two megacities—cities with more than 10 million inhabitants (there are 44 of them worldwide)—have a combined population of over 59 million people,

←

TOKYO
(Japan)
37,732,000 inhabitants

8,231 sq. km.
4,584 people per sq. km

63.3% of the inhabitants of Italy

←

DELHI
(India)
32,226,000 inhabitants

2,344 sq. km.
13,749 people per sq. km.

54.1% of the inhabitants of Italy

→

JAKARTA
(Indonesia)
33,756,000 inhabitants

3,546 sq. km.
9,521 people per sq. km.

56.6% of the inhabitants of Italy

→

NEW YORK METRO AREA
(USA)
21,509,000 inhabitants

12,093 sq. km.
1,779 people per sq. km.

36.1% of the inhabitants of Italy

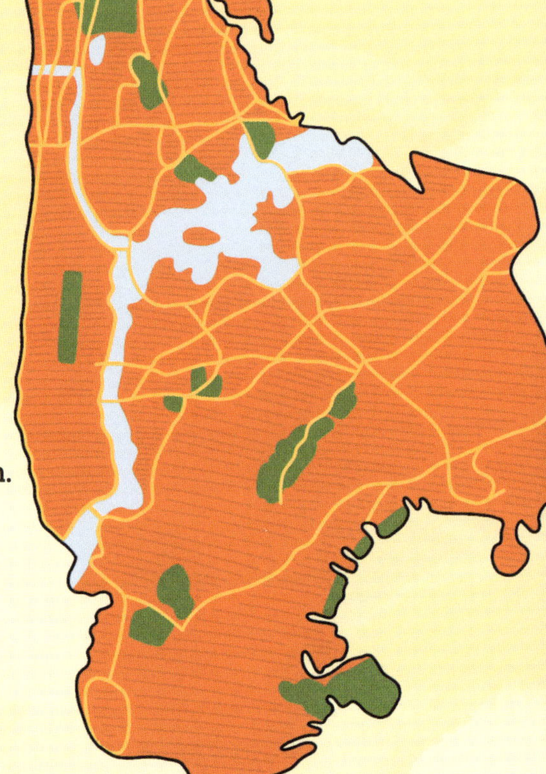

roughly the same as Italy's! Now imagine how the residents of **Hum**, a tiny town in Croatia, would react. Measuring just 330 feet (100 meters) long from one end to another, it has about **as many people as a school classroom**—just 30 inhabitants. As with countries, though, the biggest cities aren't always the most populous. New York City's metropolitan area covers more land than the **entire Abruzzo region of Italy**, making it the largest urban area by surface area. But it's not the most densely populated. On average, New York's metro area **has the equivalent of just 13 people per soccer field**. Now compare that to **Manhattan**, where skyscrapers pack people in tightly—here, the density jumps to **206 people per soccer field**. That's still far less than Dhaka, the world's most densely populated city, which crams over 30,000 people into every square kilometer (78,000 per square mile)!

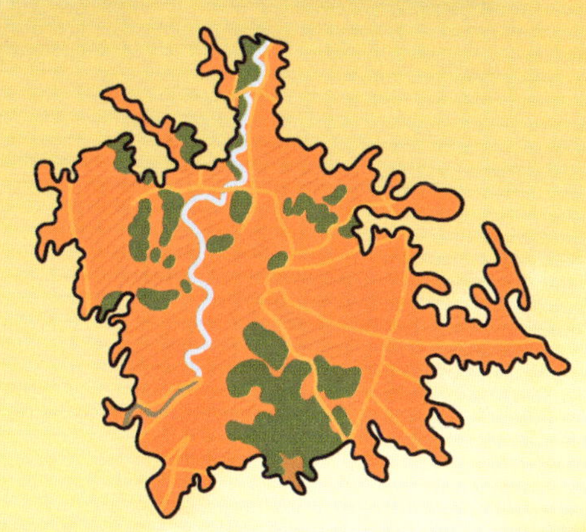

↑ ROME
(Italy)
3,214,000 inhabitants

1,145 sq. km.
2,808 people per sq. km.

5.3% of the inhabitants of Italy

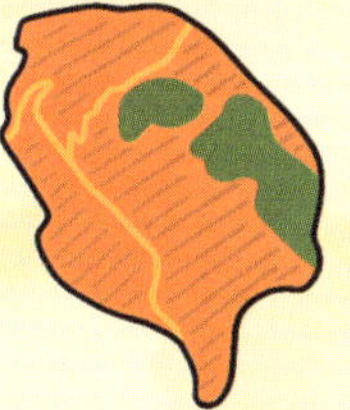

← LA PAZ
(Bolivia)
1,943,000 inhabitants

350 sq. km.
5,557 people per sq. km.

3.2% of the inhabitants of Italy

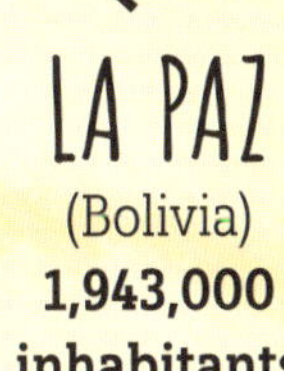

← DHAKA
(Bangladesh)
18,627,000 inhabitants

619 sq. km.
30,093 people per sq. km.

31.2% of the inhabitants of Italy

LIVING AT THE TOP OF THE WORLD

La Paz, Bolivia, has only 1/17 of the inhabitants of Jakarta, but what makes it unique is its altitude—the city sits at 11,942 feet (3,640 meters) above sea level, making it the highest capital city in the world. But the residents of nearby El Alto, Bolivia, live at 13,616 feet (4,150 meters)— as high as the peak of Italy's Gran Paradiso (13,324 feet or 4,061 meters). Even higher up, the people of La Rinconada, Peru, live at a staggering 16,732 feet (5,100 meters)—higher than Mont Blanc (15,776 feet or 4,806 meters), the tallest mountain in Western Europe!

COMPARISONS

WHAT'S LONGER: THE GREAT WALL OF CHINA OR ALL THE BLOOD VESSELS IN THE HUMAN BODY? DOES A MOSQUITO WEIGH MORE OR LESS THAN A SNOWFLAKE? MATTERS GET REALLY INTERESTING WHEN YOU START COMPARING TOTALLY DIFFERENT CATEGORIES. WHO WOULD EVER HAVE GUESSED, FOR INSTANCE, THAT THERE ARE BIRDS WITH WINGSPANS BROAD ENOUGH FOR A CAR TO FIT UNDERNEATH?

HOW BIG IS IT?

If you thought millimeters, kilometers, and everything in between (and all the other systems of measurement) were enough to measure everything there is, it's time to think again. In the world of atoms, molecules, and red blood cells, we use picometers, nanometers, and micrometers—the latter being one millionth as big as a meter. But when we scale up to planets, stars, and galaxies, we need even bigger units: the megameter (1,000 km / 621 miles), the gigameter (1 million km / 621,371 miles),

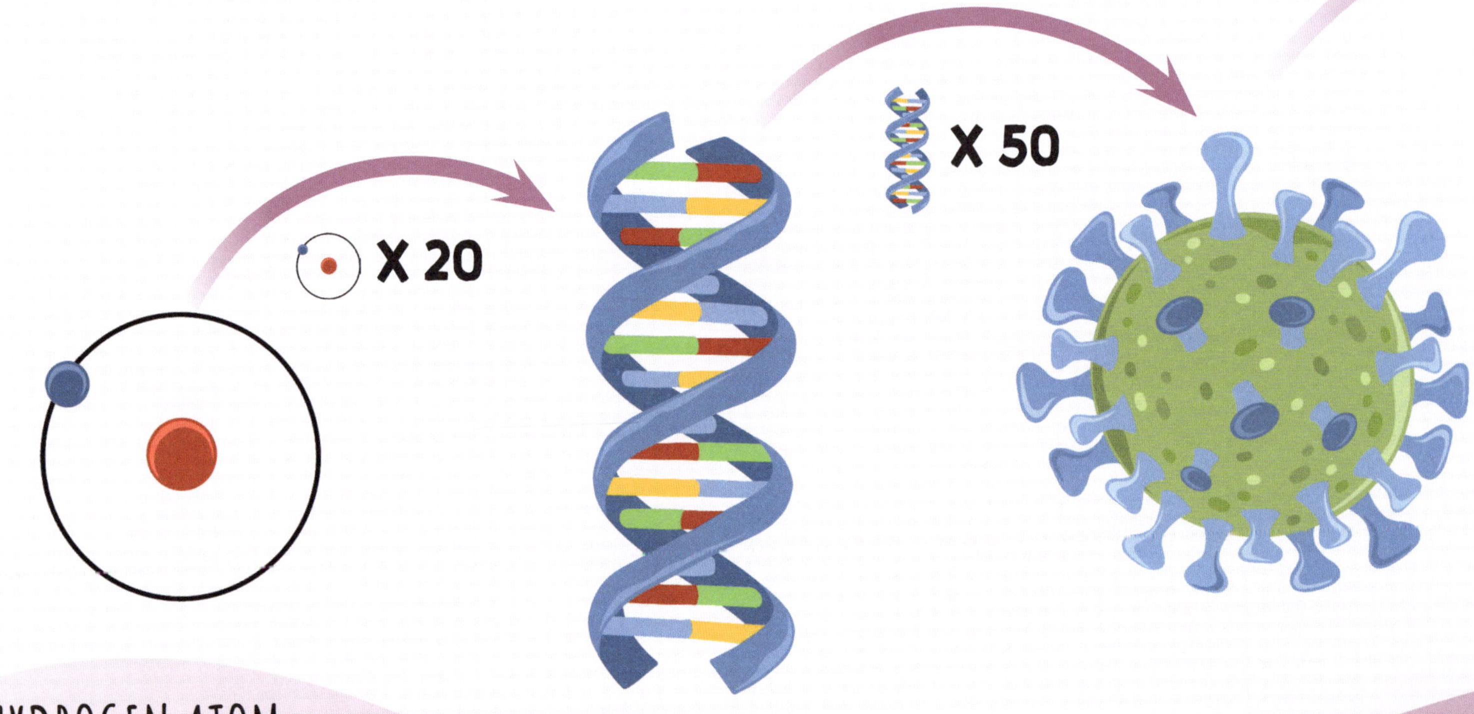

HYDROGEN ATOM

The diameter is roughly 0.1 nanometers

About 750,000 times thinner than a human hair (0.075 mm)

Hydrogen is the most abundant element in the universe.

DNA

The diameter is 2 nanometers

About 50,000 times thinner than a sheet of paper (0.1 mm)

DNA contains the genetic instructions for all living creatures on Earth. Its double helix shape resembles a party streamer: a spiraling ribbon when unraveled.

COVID-19 VIRUS

The diameter is roughly 100 nanometers (ranging from 80 to 120 nm)

5,000 times smaller than a grain of sand (0.5 mm)

Viruses come in various sizes. Some, like the Pithovirus, discovered in Siberia in 2014, can be as large as 500 nanometers in diameter.

INCREASING

and the petameter (1 trillion km / 621 billion miles), the light-year (the distance light travels in a year = 9.46 petameters / 5.88 trillion miles). But just what do these numbers actually mean? How many viruses could fit inside a grain of sand? Is the Great Wall of China longer or shorter than the Andes? Read the following pages to find out!

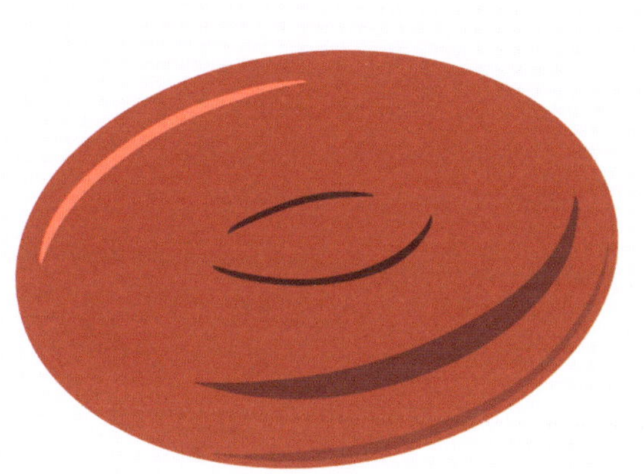

RED BLOOD CELL

The diameter is roughly 7.5 micrometers

40 times smaller than a dust mite (0.3 mm) and 133 times smaller than the thickness of a fingernail (1 mm)

Red blood cells give blood its color and transport oxygen from the lungs to the organs that need it.

FLEA

The length is roughly 3 mm

About the same diameter as a bucatini pasta noodle

3 mm

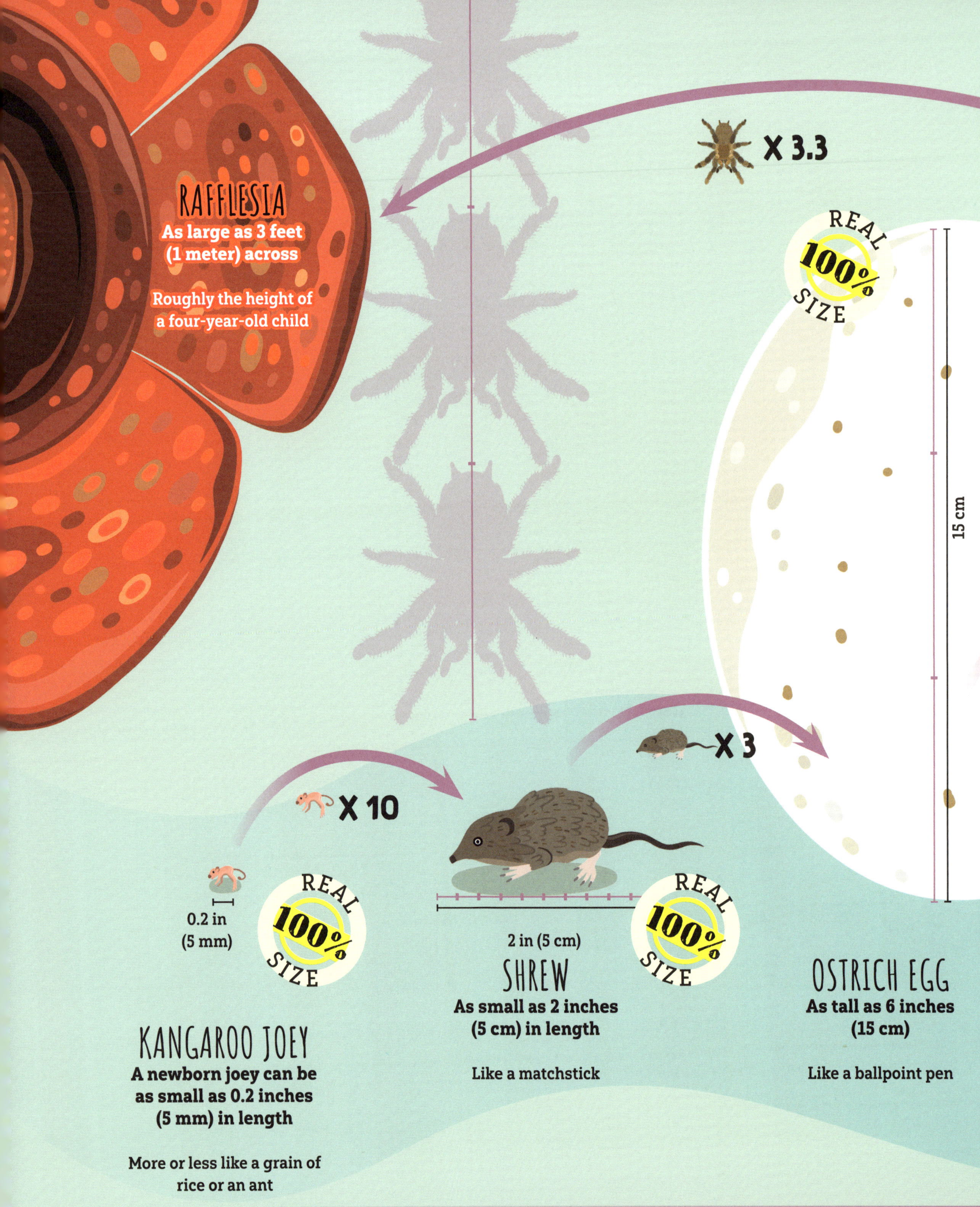

RAFFLESIA

As large as 3 feet (1 meter) across

Roughly the height of a four-year-old child

KANGAROO JOEY

A newborn joey can be as small as 0.2 inches (5 mm) in length

More or less like a grain of rice or an ant

SHREW

As small as 2 inches (5 cm) in length

Like a matchstick

OSTRICH EGG

As tall as 6 inches (15 cm)

Like a ballpoint pen

INCREASING

GOLIATH BIRDEATER

As large as a foot (30 cm) across (legs included)

Like a pizza

MONTEZUMA CYPRESS
It can have a diameter of over 46 feet (14 meters).
The length of a city bus or a whale shark
X 2.3
X 1,6
SNOWY ALBATROSS
Its wingspan can be as broad as 12 feet (3.7 meters).
Roughly the length of a compact car
This is the bird with the largest wingspan: it is constantly in flight and only stops on land when having young. For humans, the record for arm span, or reach, is over 8 feet (2.5 meters).
GIRAFFE
Male giraffes can be as tall as 20 feet (6 meters).
Like a two-story house
INCREASING

BOEING 747-8 AIRLINER

It's 250 feet long (76 meters).

Roughly the length of 3 tennis courts

X 2

X 2.6

ARGENTINOSAURUS

It could be as long as 120 feet (37 meters).

Like the Space Shuttle

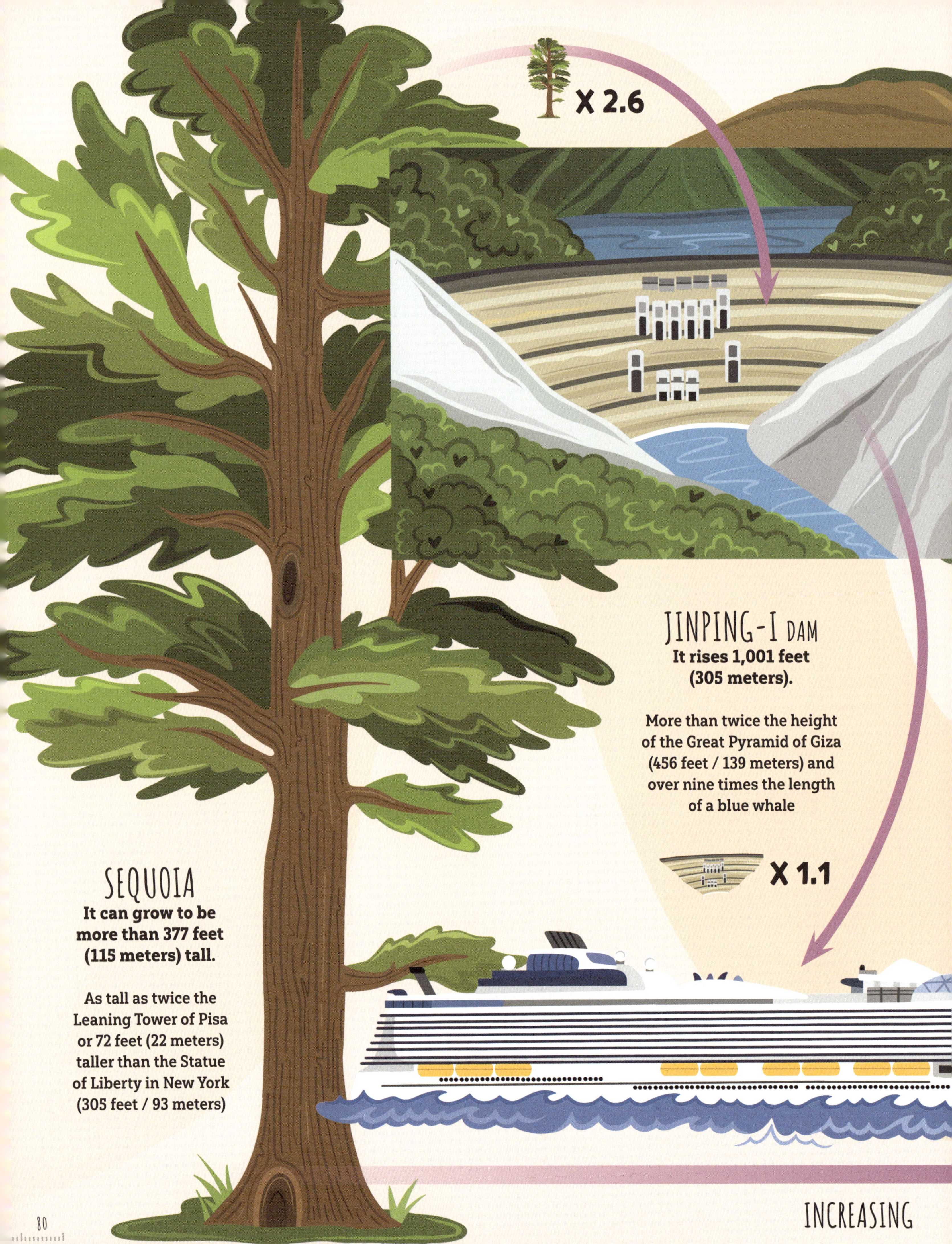
X 2.6
JINPING-I DAM
It rises 1,001 feet
(305 meters).
More than twice the height
of the Great Pyramid of Giza
(456 feet / 139 meters) and
over nine times the length
of a blue whale
X 1.1
SEQUOIA
It can grow to be
more than 377 feet
(115 meters) tall.
As tall as twice the
Leaning Tower of Pisa
or 72 feet (22 meters)
taller than the Statue
of Liberty in New York
(305 feet / 93 meters)
INCREASING

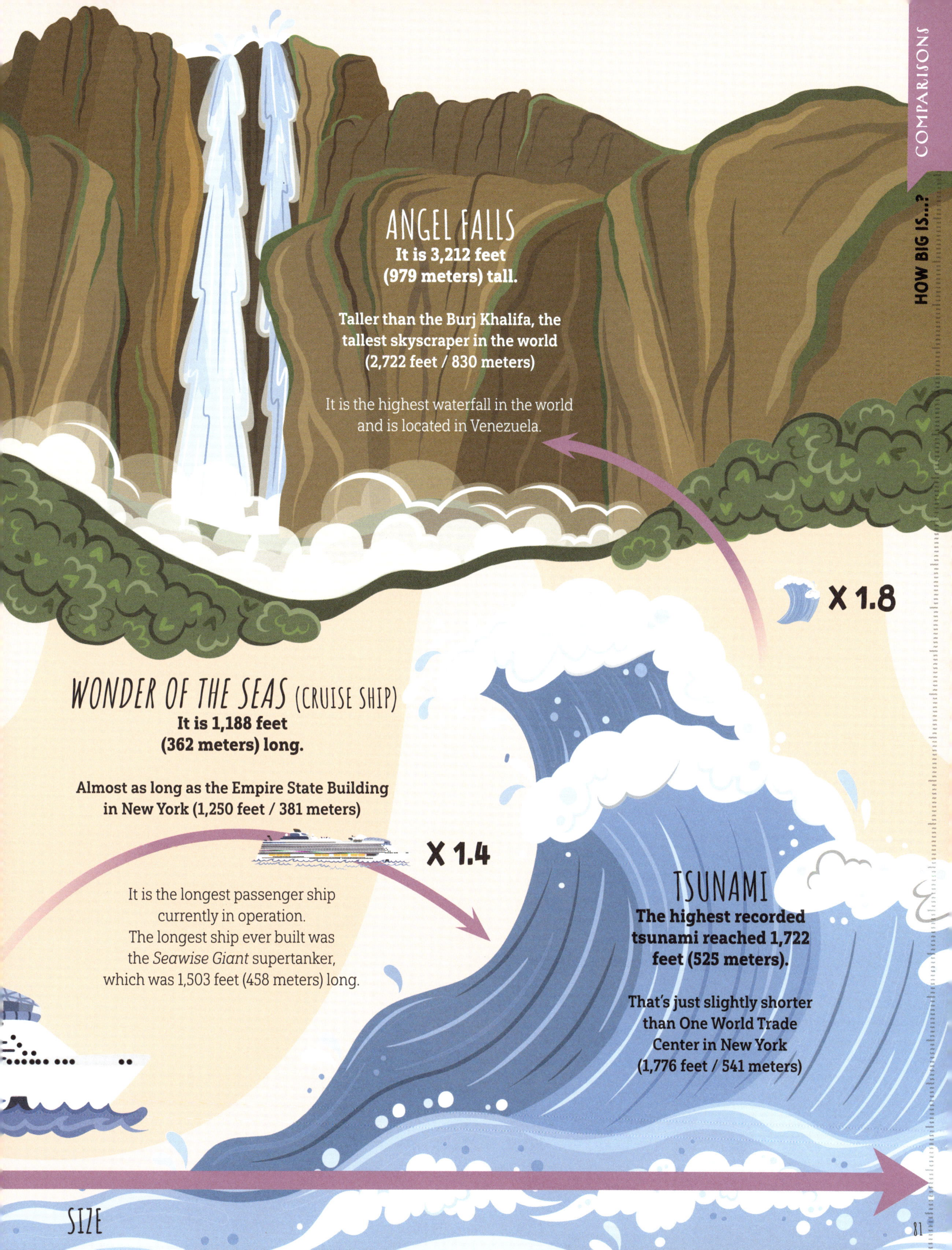

ANGEL FALLS

It is 3,212 feet (979 meters) tall.

Taller than the Burj Khalifa, the tallest skyscraper in the world (2,722 feet / 830 meters)

It is the highest waterfall in the world and is located in Venezuela.

WONDER OF THE SEAS (CRUISE SHIP)

It is 1,188 feet (362 meters) long.

Almost as long as the Empire State Building in New York (1,250 feet / 381 meters)

It is the longest passenger ship currently in operation. The longest ship ever built was the *Seawise Giant* supertanker, which was 1,503 feet (458 meters) long.

TSUNAMI

The highest recorded tsunami reached 1,722 feet (525 meters).

That's just slightly shorter than One World Trade Center in New York (1,776 feet / 541 meters)

X 1.3
ANGKOR WAT
It is approximately one mile (1.5 km) long, including the moat that surrounds it.
That's about 4.5 times the height of the Eiffel Tower.
INCREASING SIZE

DARDANELLES BRIDGE

Its main span is 1.26 miles (2.023 km) long.

That's slightly less than the diameter of Typhoon Tip, the largest and most intense typhoon ever recorded (1.38 miles / 2.220 km).

X 13.3

LARGE HADRON COLLIDER

It is 16.8 miles (27 km) long.

That's more than three times the height of Mount Everest (5.5 miles / 8,848 meters).

It is a long underground tunnel equipped with powerful magnets, built 328 feet (100 meters) underground between France and Switzerland, allowing scientists to study the smallest particles in existence.

X 85.1

X 2.8

GREAT BARRIER REEF

It stretches for 1,400 miles (2,300 km).

That's more than half the width of the United States, from its westernmost to easternmost points (2,800 miles / 4,506 km).

Taken as a whole, it is considered the largest living structure on Earth.

NILE RIVER

It is 4,100 miles (6,650 km) long.

That's more than half the diameter of the Earth (7,900 miles / 12,700 km).

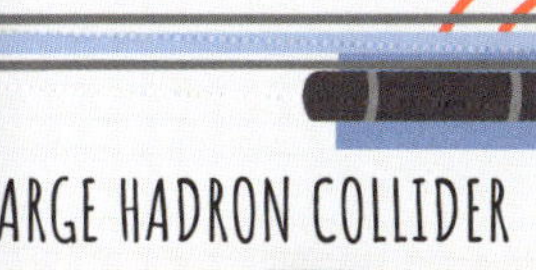

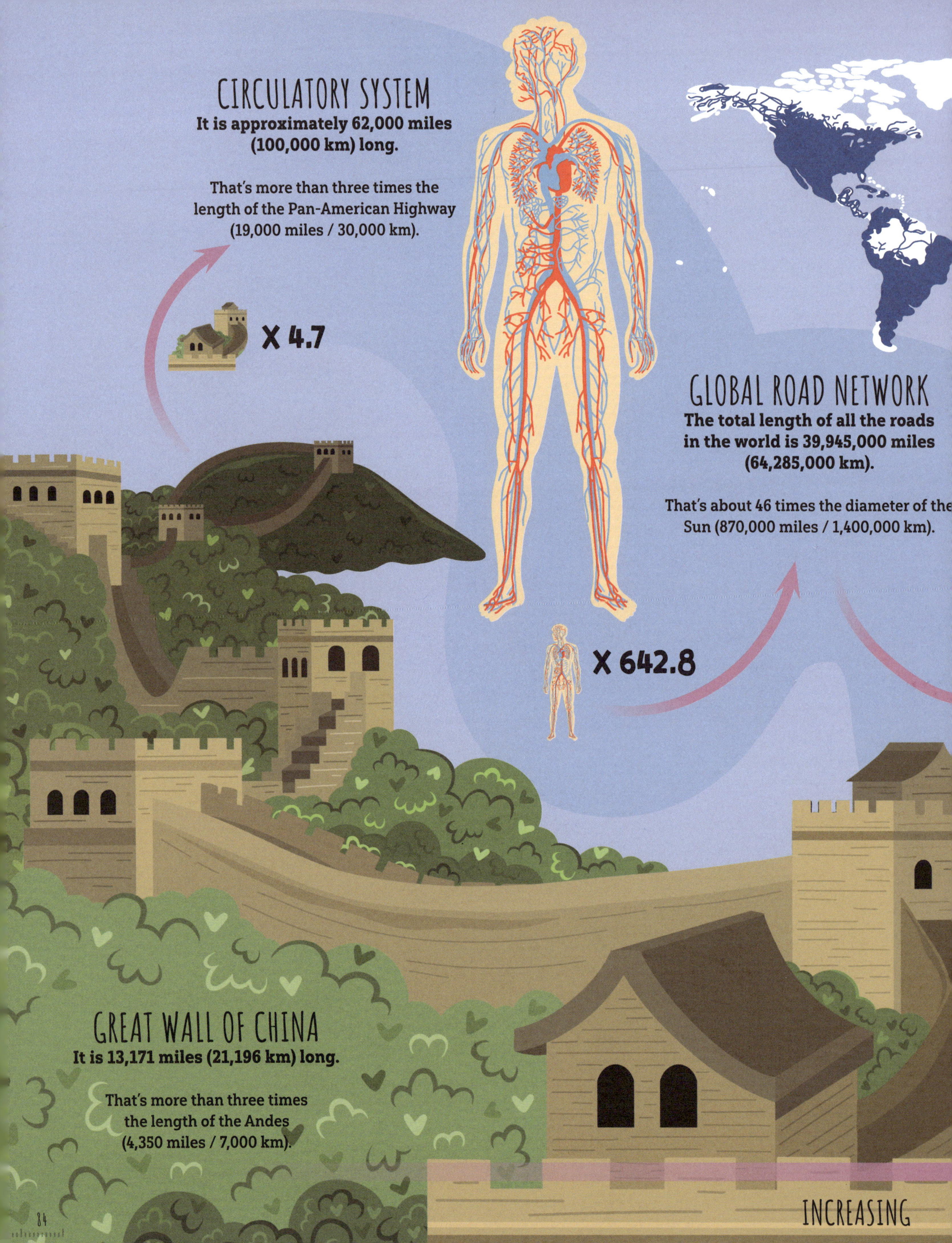
CIRCULATORY SYSTEM
It is approximately 62,000 miles (100,000 km) long.
That's more than three times the length of the Pan-American Highway (19,000 miles / 30,000 km).
X 4.7
GLOBAL ROAD NETWORK
The total length of all the roads in the world is 39,945,000 miles (64,285,000 km).
That's about 46 times the diameter of the Sun (870,000 miles / 1,400,000 km).
X 642.8
GREAT WALL OF CHINA
It is 13,171 miles (21,196 km) long.
That's more than three times the length of the Andes (4,350 miles / 7,000 km).
INCREASING

MILKY WAY

Its diameter is 120,000 light-years, which equals over one quintillion miles (705 quadrillion miles / 1,135,287,656,709,605,200 km).

The Earth's diameter is 90 trillion times smaller—comparable to the size difference between a flea and more than 14 million Great Walls of China.

We are here, in one of the over 200 billion galaxies known to exist in the universe.

KUIPER BELT

It extends for 9 billion miles (15 billion km).

That's like traveling to Mars and back 3,282 times.

It is a disk-shaped region located beyond Neptune's orbit, at the edge of our solar system. It is filled with asteroids, comets, and other celestial bodies.

HOW FAST IS...?

VARIEGATED SLOTH
0.16 mph
(0.25 km/h)

X 16

HUMAN WALKING
2.5 mph
(4 km/h)

X 1.8

HOUSEFLY
4.5 mph
(7.2 km/h)

X 6.

X 1.3

MAGLEV TRAIN
375 mph
(603 km/h)

X 1.32

TSUNAMI
497 mph
(800 km/h)

X 1.56

COMMERCIAL AIRLINER
776 mph
(1,249 km/h)

X 46.4

ROCKETSHIP
ATLAS V/NEW HORIZONS ROCKET
36,000 mph (58,000 km/h)

X 4.3

METEORITE
155,000 mph
(250,000 km/h)

X 2.7

PARKER SOLAR PROBE
430,000 mph
692,000 km/h

HUMAN RUNNING
27 mph
(44 km/h)
Usain Bolt, the fastest man on earth

X 1.6

ELEVATOR
46 mph
(74 km/h)
Shanghai Tower Elevator

X 1.4

PASSENGER SHIP
67 mph (107 km/h)

X 1.19

CHEETAH
80 mph (128 km/h)

X 2.6

HURRICANE PATRICIA
214 mph
(345 km/h)

X 1.13

PEREGRINE FALCON
242 mph (390 km/h)

X 1.14

RODUCTION CAR
278 mph
(447 km/h)

X 1559

SPEED OF LIGHT
670,600,000 mph
(1,079,000,000 km/h)

HOW MUCH DOES IT WEIGH?

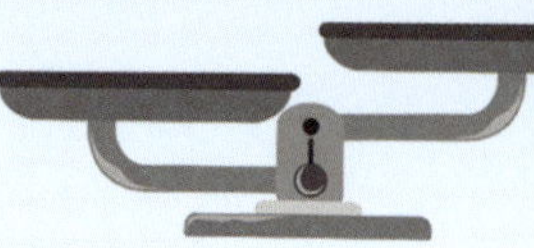

AS LIGHT AS...

A MOSQUITO
0.00009 ounce (0.0025 gram)

Slightly less than a snowflake (0.0001 ounces / 0.003 g)

X 3,000

A ONE-EURO COIN
0.26 ounce (7.5 grams)

Like three bee hummingbirds (0.09 ounces / 2.5 g)

X 2.8

A MOUSE
0.74 ounce (21 grams)

Like four sheets of paper (0.17 ounces / 4.9 g)

X 1.7

AS HEAVY AS...

AN OSTRICH
340 pounds (150 kg)

Like an upright piano

X 8.3

A SALTWATER CROCODILE
2,900 pounds (1,300 kg)

Like a small car

X 116

A BULLDOZER
Komatsu D575A-3
335,000 pounds (152,000 kg)

Like 21 T-Rexes (15,432 pounds / 7,000 kg) or 1.5 Argentinosauruses

X 2.9

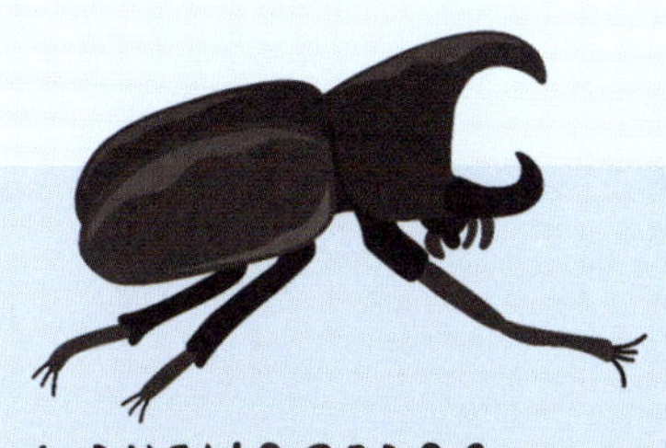

A RHINOCEROS BEETLE

1.3 ounces (36 grams)

Like three AAA batteries

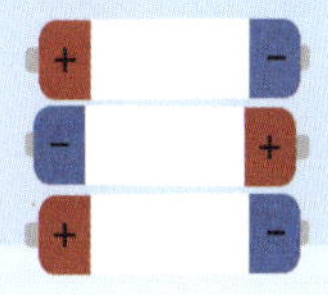

X 1.6

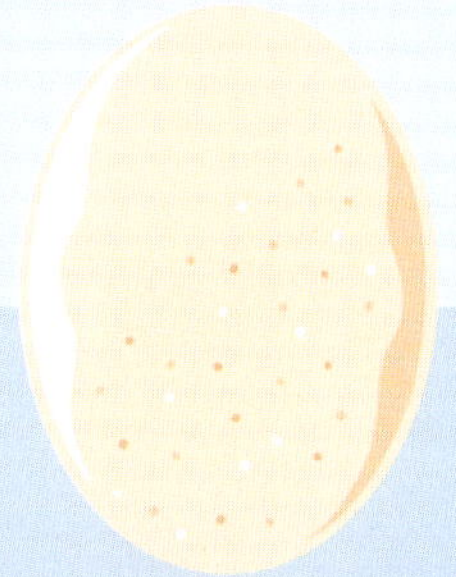

A CHICKEN EGG

2 ounces (60 grams)

Like a tennis ball

X 15

GIANT AFRICAN SNAIL

32 ounces (900 grams)

Like nine newborn kittens

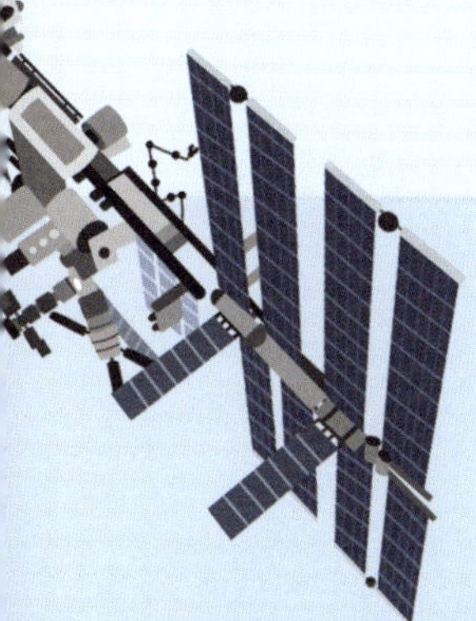

ISS

971,500 pounds (440,700 kg)

More than two blue whales

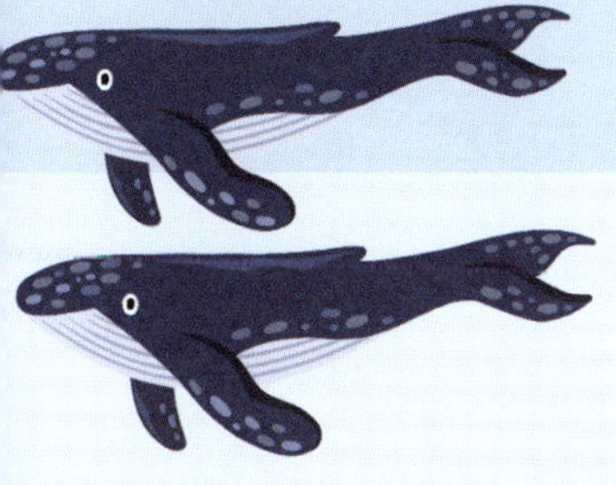

X 30.6

AN EXCAVATOR

Bagger 288

30,000,000 pounds (13,500,000 kg)

Almost like five Saturn V rockets filled with fuel

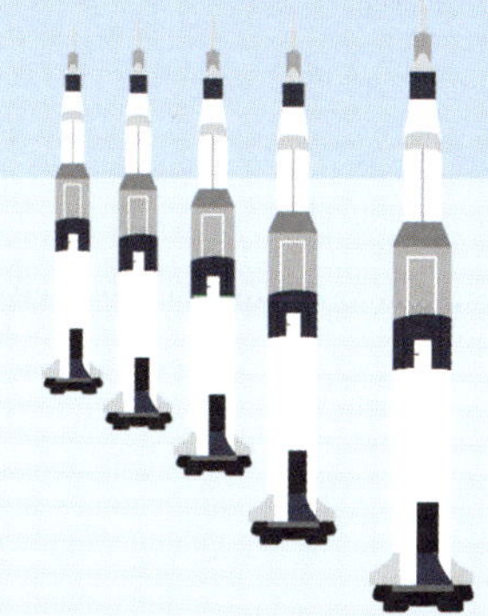

X 303

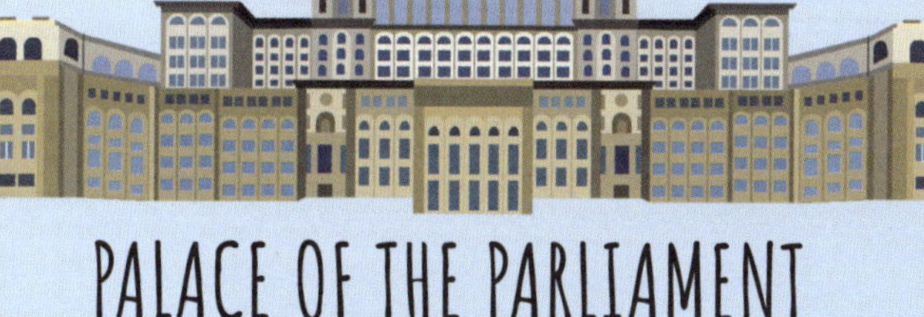

PALACE OF THE PARLIAMENT IN BUCHAREST

9,035,461,000 pounds (4,098,500,000 kg)

Like the entire population of Italy

ECOLOGY

NATURAL RESOURCES

1.7 is the number of Earth-like planets we would need to make up for the quantity of natural resources we consume each year.

In 1971, the day humankind exhausted the Earth's annual sustainable natural resources was December 25. In 2022, it happened much earlier—on July 28.

DIGITAL POLLUTION

2.5 hours of a streaming movie or video-call produces about the same amount of CO_2 as **a car burning a quart (1 liter) of gasoline.**

QUANTITY OF PLASTIC WASTE

441 million short tons (400 million metric tons) of plastic waste are produced every year, of which at least 10 million short tons (9 million metric tons) end up in the oceans—**equivalent to almost 50,000 blue whales.**

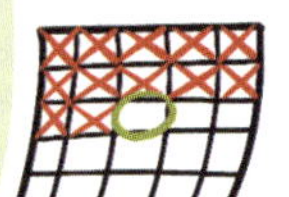

FOOD WASTE

1 billion short tons (931 million metric tons) of food are wasted every year—**about 163 lbs (74 kg) per person.**

MEAT CONSUMPTION

Producing 2.2 lbs (1 kg) of beef requires over 4,000 gallons (15,000 liters) of water—**the equivalent of 83 bathtubs**.

In comparison: it takes only 85 gallons (322 liters) of water to grow 2.2 lbs (1 kg) of vegetables. And it takes only 434 gallons (1,644 liters) of water to grow 2.2 lbs (1 kg) of grains.

In 1961, average global meat consumption was 53 lbs (24 kg) per person per year. Today, that number has risen to 97 lbs (44 kg) per person per year.

The territories that consume the most meat per capita are as follows: Hong Kong: 302 lbs (137 kg); United States: 274 lbs (124 kg); Australia: 267 lbs (121 kg); Argentina: 243 lbs (110 kg); Spain, Brazil, and Israel: about 220 lbs (100 kg); and Italy: 180 lbs (81 kg).

TEMPERATURE

Since 1880, in about 140 years, the Earth's average temperature has increased by about 1°C (1.8°F). The 19 hottest years on record have all occurred since the year 2000.

The highest temperature ever recorded was **134.1°F (56.7°C)** in Death Valley, USA. The lowest temperature ever recorded was **-128.6°F (-89.2°C)** in Antarctica.

RISING SEA LEVELS

Over the past 30 years, global sea levels have risen by approximately 4 inches (10 cm), increasing by about 0.13 inches (3.4 mm) per year.

It is estimated that 630 million people live in countries that, by the year 2100, will be flooded—roughly the same as **the entire populations of Brazil, the United States, and Russia combined.**

ICE LOSS

Since 2002, over a period of 20 years, the amount of ice lost in Antarctica and Greenland has totaled 9.4 trillion short tons (8.5 trillion metric tons)—about 471 billion US tons (427 billion metric tons) per year, or enough to fill approximately **⅓ of Lake Como.**

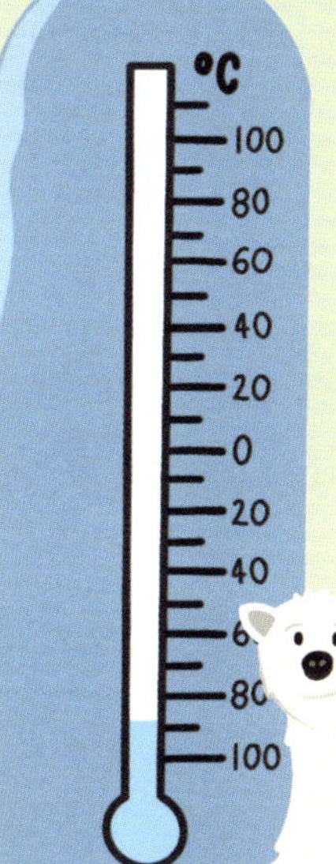

HOW MANY MORE YEARS WOULD WE LIVE IF THE AIR WERE CLEANER?

How many years of life would we gain if air pollution remained within the limits set by the World Health Organization (WHO)? That was the question a research team at the University of Chicago sought to answer by developing an interactive world map (The Air Quality Life Index), where pollution levels and life expectancy loss can be seen for each region. The most polluted areas on Earth are found in India, in cities like **Delhi**, where air pollution is estimated to reduce **life expectancy by up to 10 years.** In some parts of **Cameroon** (Africa) and **China**, the estimated loss is 5 years. In Europe, the situation is perhaps better, but the most polluted areas are in Bosnia and Herzegovina (2.3 years lost), Poland (1.5 years lost), and Italy (Po Valley region, including Milan, Brescia, and Turin—more than 1 year of life lost).

INDEX

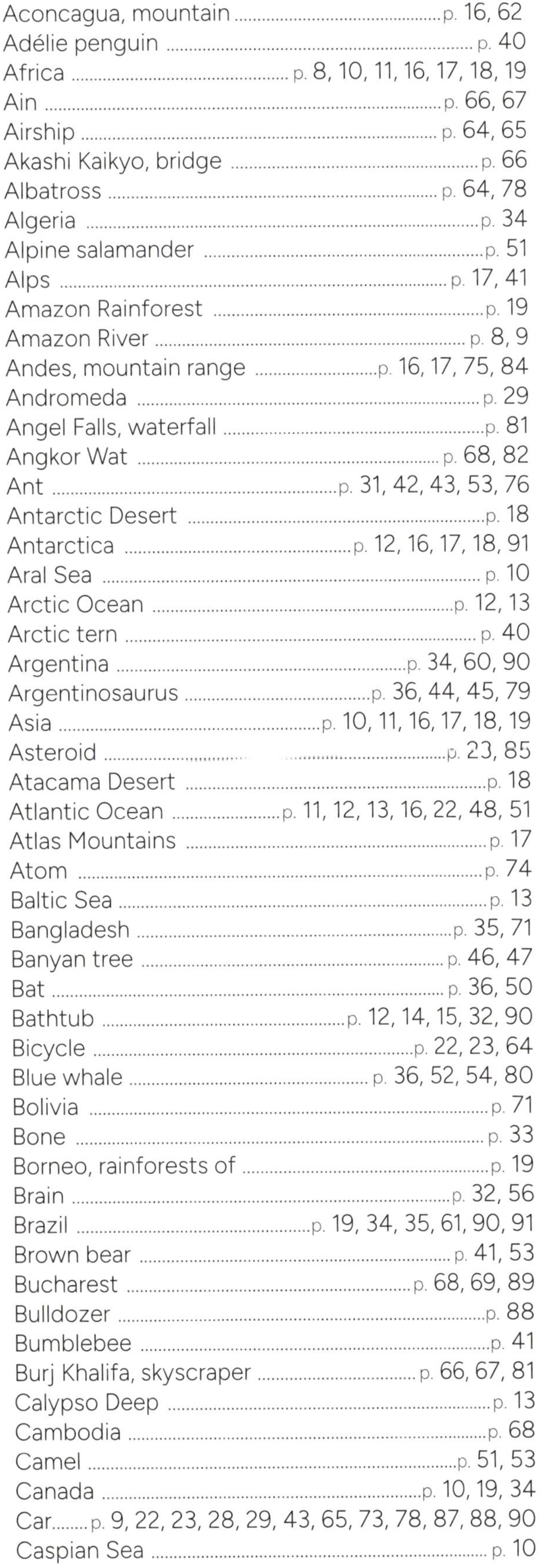